Embraced by the Father's Love

Brian Fenimore

Plumbline Ministries
Belton, Mo

Published by Plumbline Publishing
From Plumbline Ministries
Belton, Mo. U.S.A.
www.plumbline.me
Printed in the U.S.A.

All Scripture quotations, unless otherwise indicated, are taken from the New American Standard Bible, by the Lockman Foundation ®. Used by permission.

Copyright ® 2018 Brian Fenimore
All rights reserved. No part of this publication may be reproduced. Stored in a retrieval system or transmitted in any form by any means, electronic, mechanical, photocopy, recording or otherwise, without the prior permission of the publisher, except as provided by USA copyright law.

Contents

Chapter One..5
The Embrace of God

Chapter Two...33
The Embrace of the Father

Chapter Three..64
The Compassion of God

Chapter Four.. ..103
The Mercy Throne of God

Chapter Five..135
The Spirit of Adoption

Books By **Brian Fenimore**

The voice of the Lord thunders

Foundation for prophetic ministry

Heart standard for the prophetic

Awakening the kingdom within

Advancing the Kingdom of God

Exploring spiritual gifts

Philosophy of visions

Bible study: Love, mercy and Grace

Chapter One

The Embrace of God

There is a lot of teaching these days on the Fatherhood of God, but there is not nearly as much of what I call foundational teaching about it. Usually it's more like "Hey, God's your Father. He loves you." Most of us know this intellectually, but we need to have some additional foundation laid in this area that the Spirit can utilize to go deeper in us, emotionally and spiritually. When we begin to understand and then experience God as a Father, it actually changes our whole walk as a Christian.

There is a blessing in knowing Jesus as our Savior

and as our Friend but Jesus wants to do more than that for us. He wants to introduce us to His Father. He wants us to know Him as a Father, and it's very important that our lives are touched by this concept of God being a Father. This goes deeper than having just intellectual assent but really experiencing it so that it transforms us spiritually and emotionally.

FATHERING AS DEFINED IN PSALMS 68

We're going to look at many of Bible verses expressing the truth about God's nature as a Father as we go forward.

"A father of the fatherless and a judge for the widows, is God in his holy habitation. God makes a home for the lonely, and he leads out the prisoners into prosperity." (**Psalms 68:5,6**)

This scripture tells us that for people who are fatherless, God becomes a Father. So let's define what it means to be a father a bit further. There are two ways the Scripture uses the term father.
First, the term father means the originator of life. In

the truest sense of the word, even though we have earthly fathers and earthly mothers who He utilized in pro-creation, God Himself is the originator of our life. He's our first and forever Father. That's important to know, that the Originator of our being on this planet, the One who intentionally created us is God the Father! God the Father wanted me here and He wanted you here.

We were brought into existence because He wants to be our Father, and He fathered us in the truest sense of the word. Even though our parents might have been the biological agents, God decided we were going to be who we were going to be. He fathered each of us in the ultimate sense.

Second, God is our Father in the idea of modeling. This is very important. A lot of children realize that their earthly father is the origin or the originator of their biological life, but they have an immature modeling of fatherhood regarding Him. So when they hear things like, "God is our Heavenly Father," they think something like, "Oh, that means He must be like my earthly father. He gave origin to me, but then he took off and went on vacation or something, and there's no interaction or nurturing going on in terms of him and me." So while the idea of father means originator of life, that's certainly not all that's going on in a biblical sense. It also means being a model of nurture in life.

God being a Father affects both men and women, especially as it concerns this concept of nurturing. If someone has had a perception of an absence of God nurturing them in their life, the concept of Him being a Father may be a mere intellectual exercise so as to align in theory with scriptural teaching but can be absolutely foreign to them in everyday, practical reality.

God is faithful and He is determined to integrate His embracing of our life in such a way that prosperity (the word prosperity means wholeness) - comes into every part of us. God's determined desire is to restore wholeness of fathering over us and within us.

FATHERS AS PRIESTS
Let's look at an example in the Bible of this idea of

nurturing. It is out of an obscure passage in the book of Judges. *"'I am a Levite of Bethlehem of Judea, and I am going to sojourn where I might find a place.' Micaiah said to him, 'Well, stay with me and be to me a father and a priest, and I will give you a tenth piece of silver a year and a suit of clothes for your living.' The Levite went and stayed with him. The Levite was content to dwell with the man, and the young man became to him like one of his sons".*(**Judges 17: 9,10**)

The whole idea of God being a Father and the role for men as fathers are both contained in being a priest. This is very significant. Because I had no religious training as a child, the picture that would usually come up in my imagination was of a Catholic church where they walk around wearing vestments, and waving incense around, and people sip from a cup and take a little wafer from them.

There's no interaction or modeling involved. That's a ceremonial function of a priest in a certain context. Actually, a priest in scripture is really interesting because the first foundational truth of being a priest is to carry someone in your heart. A fuller sense of the biblical meaning of being a priest shows what it is to be a father who does much more than be an initiator of life. Being a priest means someone that carries another person continually.

God being a Father is this idea of not just bringing us into existence, but of carrying us in His heart, of having a continuous desire to always look over our life to see if we are prospering. He also sees that we are doing well and that we are flourishing as individuals. The reality of the Greek word sozo, as Christ taught It is, what we call salvation in the English language.

It is very important when it comes to God being a Father. Too many of us, when God favors us or blesses us, can tend to have an attitude something like, "Oh, I guess that's God," but they aren't really sure if it is God or not. But in fact, God is trying to communicate something through every action He does in our lives.

The action that He is trying to communicate, not only that He is God and He is able to do these things, but He does them for a purpose and a reason. The reason is that <u>we are on His heart, and He is intentionally trying to show us acts of personal kindness as expressions of love.</u> He is communicating <u>directly to us saying, "I am Your Father who nurtures and cares about you."</u>

REALIZING GOD AS OUR FATHER TRANSFORMS OUR PRAYER LIFE

For the first ten years that I walked with the Lord, I was just trying to figure out how prayer works so I could get answers to prayer. In the middle of that pursuit, the Lord began to challenge me that answers to prayer were good, but that wasn't the only reason, or even the main reason God answers prayer.

Another reason that God answers prayer is that He desires to connect with our hearts. My heart was frozen or dead to the concept that God wanted to nurture me as my Father. One of the main ways He was demonstrating this to me was He constantly interacting in my life and answering prayers in my life to hopefully convince me of His nurturing as a Father. If we haven't had this modeled to us when God is acting like Himself by fathering the fatherless, then we will tend to misunderstand His intent. If we don't see this as God being nurturing, we will interpret it as something it isn't, and our heart remains cold to the idea that God wants to be a Father to us.

THE PROPHECY AND PROMISE OF MALACHI 4:5,6

We live in an interesting generation. I have never seen so much fragmentation of family and the family structure throughout the world. Men are growing up without a father, many women have no men successfully modeling fathering to children, just broken men trying to take on the roles of trying to act like fathers when they have no modeling and really don't know how very well. There is such a desperate cry for God to be a Father and fathering to be done properly in our society today. It's just unbelievable how much this is needed.

In the book of Malachi, it talks about Elijah coming again. If you talk to Jewish people, they say, "This means that Elijah will actually show up someday." Protestants say, "Well, it's not Elijah coming back on Earth and working miracles again, it's the spirit of

Elijah." The focus I have here isn't any of that. I'm more fascinated about what it says about what will happen when Elijah comes again." It says that when Elijah comes again: *"And he will restore the heart of the fathers to the children, and the heart of the children to their fathers"* (**Malachi 4:6**). Isn't that interesting? The ministry of Elijah demonstrated such powerful miracles of the Lord. Just imagine.

That same spirit is going to come again on a generation during the end-times, and what it will do is restore healthy father-children, children-father relationships at every level. It is going to be a restoration of us towards God the Father and us being proper fathers and fathering children correctly. That is going to be one of the most significant signs of the end of the age. It seems almost everybody is looking for the mark of the beast as a huge sign of the end. But let me share something with you.

The mark of the beast and trying to figure out the identity of the anti-Christ is largely a waste of time, at least in the way too many of us are going about it. A far better sign on which to be focused is the coming of the spirit of Elijah in restoring the hearts of children to their Father. This is a sign and a promise that God is going to come in a very powerful way and restore proper nurturing to people again.

"YOU ARE MY SUNSHINE" SAID HER FATHER-GOD

A congregation contacted me a while back and said, "Would you mind coming and praying for our staff?" I said, "Well, sure. I'd be glad to do so." At the same time that I went there, my mother-in-law had open heart surgery. So my wife Kellie and I are traveling there. Then my mom has a friend who has to be admitted into the emergency room.

So I have all this external stuff swirling around me as I go forward to minister to a group of people. I went to stay with my mother-in-law, and since her children have moved on with their lives and out of her house, she's gotten rid of all the extra beds there. So there's only one bed for anybody, and Kellie came with me. I felt it was necessary that Kellie slept on the bed, and I slept on the floor. Have you ever slept on the floor recently? It's really a lot of fun, it really does a number and not in a good way, on your back. I needed to get up at five the next morning so I went bed. I got up at five and drove back to Denver, from Pueblo, Colorado, after being at the emergency room in Pueblo all day the day before. Then I had an appointment to meet a group and ended up doing ministry for seven hours.

I was tired because I really didn't get much sleep. Also I had severe pain in my body. I came into a room of 30 or 40 people that wanted me to pray for them and just started praying. I get to the end of the people wanting me to minister to them, and as I'm coming up to the last person there's something really interesting that God is doing. I'm being filled with joy and I hear a song in my head. A lot of songs that are written and God can use them because of the lyrics to actually speak to people.

Not all of them of course, because some of them are so wicked. So there's no way God would ever use those, but some songs He chooses to use.

As I'm looking at this lady, I hear this phrase, "Brian, I want you to sing this song to this woman." Then I hear the song, "You are my sunshine, my only sunshine. You make me happy when skies are grey. You'll never know dear, how much I love you. Please don't take your sunshine away." I say back to Him, "I am not going to sing that song, God." I even said to the Lord, "That's not – yeah, I know that's not You," and so I just ignored it.

As I got closer to her, every time I looked at her, this joy would fill my heart and then I'd hear the song, "You are my sunshine, my..." Okay. I'm not going to sing it right now because singing is not one of my abilities. If I ever sing really well, you know the anointing of the Lord is on me.

I got to where she was in line and she's standing there to receive prayer. I said, "You know, I keep asking the Lord to give me something different to share with you, but He's not. All I'm getting is a song." I said, "I'm kind of embarrassed to sing it because I'm not a good singer, so I'm going to just quote the song to you." Now she was looking at me like, "What is this guy going to do?" I said, "The song is this, 'You are my sunshine, my only sunshine. You make me happy when skies are grey.

You'll never know dear how much I love you. Please don't take your sunshine away.'" Doesn't that sound absolutely random like it just has nothing to do with anything? Well, she responded by buckling over and started sobbing uncontrollably to the point where everyone there looked at her thinking, "Oh, my goodness. What just happened?" All right. So with that situation I couldn't pray or anything.

Several women gathered around her and she sat there for 20 or 30 minutes, sobbing uncontrollably. Someone there may have thought she was sobbing because what I shared with her was so ridiculous. When the meeting was over it was time to go to lunch.

At lunch the associate pastor who was eating lunch with me leans over and says, "Hey, may I share with you what just happened with that lady with whom you prayed?" I said, "Well, sure." He said, "Well, that's the

Embraced by the Father's Love

pastor's wife. Last night, her husband was singing that song to their daughters. In fact, he's been singing it to her and their daughters for the last two weeks. In her heart she said to herself before the meeting, "My father never nurtured me. I have no idea what it means to have a father who would nurture me.

I wonder what it would be like if God sang that song over me." God's love is so powerful! God paying attention to this woman's plea, loving this adult daughter of His, giving someone who doesn't even think they can sing a word, revealed His Father heart to her. All of us, God's children, have been ordained for Him to do this for us. God is listening to what's going on in our life. God is listening to the things that are on our heart.

He's planning on coming and powerfully nurturing us in such a way that we're convinced of the fact that He's our Father. In fact, I think Jesus's ministry is the reason why it's so powerful. Not only did He provide salvation for us, but He provides an understanding of God as being our Father in a very powerful way. He said in effect, "He's My Father and your Father." In fact, He intentionally picked a term for father that means Papa in the original biblical language because He wanted to make sure that we understood that in God's eyes, He relates to us as a familiar, loving Papa, not a faraway Father that you could not know.

God intentionally has planned these encounters of love to model nurture to us. Let's go back to the biblical passage we've been focusing on here. It says, "God also makes a home for the lonely." Now, the term home, this could be literal in a physical sense. We would see a lot of Christian relief work comes from the fact that people have been fathered by God and then God gives them a strategy to begin to father other people. The passage itself isn't talking about that. The passage **Psalms 68:6** says, *"God makes a home."* What is the reality of God making a home for the lonely?

"I AM YOUR HOME"
We can be in a crowd of people and still be lonely. So here is a very important truth. It does not say, "God makes a place where we can go visit with people." God is addressing that deep longing in our hearts

where we feel that no one understands us. Loneliness has to do with not ever feeling like someone really knows us. God says that He makes a home for the lonely. One of the most nurturing things about God as a Father is that He wants to come and live with us, moment by moment forever.

How many of us have acknowledged this when we have walked with the Lord, that God knows us personally and individually just as if there wasn't another person in the entire world? He doesn't just tell us, "Hey, just grow up." We can tell by His dialogue and His interaction with us in our life that He knows us well. He's not afraid by who we are or who we've been. In fact, He loves who we are, and He's trying to convince us, "I like you the way you are even though you don't like yourself some of the time." Do you ever struggle with thinking, "If I could just live one day where I would be pleased with myself, then I could accept the fact that God loves me." Yet, we find out in Romans that it says; *"While we were yet sinners, Christ died for us"* (**Romans 5:8**) What this shows is that when we are at our worst,

God says, "I intentionally love you even though you're not receiving this." The love of God and this idea of God being a Father is so powerful that it literally is the most transforming truth in the world. God wants to come and take loneliness from us. Different people lead different lifestyles-- that's for sure. My lifestyle is literally on the road. I'm alone, physically alone, a lot of the time. Yet when Jesus was struggling with being alone, He said: *"And He who sent Me is with Me. He has not left Me alone"* (**John 8:29**) One of the most intense experiences I've had with loneliness is when God was in the process of trying to mold my heart.

It was a systematic breaking of my heart over a series of events. I was in Africa a few years ago for the very first time. Because of the AIDS epidemic there that had taken their parents, there were so many children living on the streets. I saw them sleeping on the side of the road. This terrible situation started to grip my heart.

It wasn't that I had never known on some level that this existed but it was right in my face and I had to deal with it on another level. I'm wrestling inside myself with the obvious question, "Where are the people who can take care of these kids? Where are the fathers here? How are these children going to have any type of quality of life or have a chance to understand God as a Father if they never have a father ever?" So I'm lying in my bed, contemplating how awful this really is.

Somehow, for some reason, I'm starting to contemplate this fact when I'm on the other side of the world from my home. And right there something happened to me. No one could help me. I realized that I was away from my family and my children, and everyone that I'd known and loved. I was becoming very aware that I was on the other side of the world while serving the Lord.

While I'm in that place feeling very vulnerable and broken, seeing and sensing this kind of destruction in a culture, God comes to me. I began to talk with Him, "Lord, I just feel so far from home and so lonely." Then He says, "Brian, you're home. You're home." He wasn't saying, "Move here." He was saying, "I'm home to you. I'm home. I'm here to meet you that you would know that you're secure and you're settled in the fact that I'm your home anywhere you happen to be." How does God deal with loneliness in a culture? He might give us a bunch of friends, but we can't be friends with people until God makes home in our hearts.

This is the idea of God embracing you, hugging you, and telling you at your weakest point that you're accepted by him. This is His beautiful role of being a father. Not only does God become the father to the fatherless and a compassionate judge for the widows, and makes a home for the lonely, but it also says, "He leads out prisoners into prosperity." So there's a reality that we can be nurtured and yet not get out of a situation or circumstance.

Do you realize that? If we are around people who are filled with compassion, they know how to show compassion and comfort other people. But a lot of times, they can't offer anything like "Well, let's get you out of this trouble." They just know how to sympathize in trouble? And that's a good thing.

But God is saying more to us than that. He's saying, "Here's what I am like in your life. I'm a Father to you, and whenever you're imprisoned, I will not only deliver you from that, I will go to the next step and make you prosper." I am all into God delivering, aren't you? Think of the trouble and trials of which God has freed us in our lives. But this is what I would call an intense expression of love. Not only does He deliver us, He doesn't leave us in the place of being delivered, He leads us into a place where our life is full of joy. It actually defines God as a Father and touches His heart to see us prosper in everything we do.

Now, this is an amazing Father who we have and with Him doing this kind of thing, He shows us what nurturing actually looks like. So for both men and women when we define, "What is parenting?" or "What does it mean to care for people well?, there is the practical reality of our Heavenly Father. It means to step into these kinds of challenges and then be empowered to begin to not only see people set free, but to see them prosper again. Let me give you an example of how God started trying to help me with this.

GETTING GENTLY HIT WITH HEALING

I had been traveling again and I got sick on the road. When I came home, I wanted my wife to pray for me. So I said, "Hey, Kellie, would you mind just laying hands on me and praying for me?" We were in our kitchen and my wife gently laid hands on me, and she said, "Jesus, help Brian." She gets done and then I was kind of frustrated that I didn't get healed instantly.

So then I said to her (and by the way this isn't a good way to respond to your wife). I said, "Could you do this again? But when you do it, could you pray like you actually believe Jesus is going to heal me this time?" Now my wife has a wonderful sense of humor so she says, "So you want me to pray like I really believe Jesus is going to heal you, huh?"
I said, "Yeah, that would really be a benefit at this particular moment." So she takes her hand, the palm of her hand, and she smacks me on the head significantly enough to get my attention.
She says, "Jesus, heal Brian right now!"
She yelled it over me and hit me on the head. I actually almost went down to the ground, and then I looked at her. Now my throat was inflamed, I mean it

was just killing me. I almost said, "Well, why did you do that?" But as I swallowed, I realized that I was healed. I got this amazed look on my face and said, "What was that?" I was so shocked that this happened that I thanked my wife and then hugged her. Then I went back to my bedroom in semi-shock, and I lay down on the bed.

Then God started showing up in a direct way to me. He said, "It's my delight to do these things. I love doing these kinds of things in your life." I can tell you this from growing up fatherless and then to be in walking with the Lord for almost 30 years now, that I have seen this rhythm and this dance and this joy that Jesus does personally with me.

FATHER-GOD WANTS TO SAVE AND PROSPER US - LIFE MORE ABUNDANT

Our Father-God is always intentionally trying to help us realize the joy He has from not only delivering us, but in prospering us. It's a wrong way to look at ourselves, Do you ever internally talk to yourself and say, "I'm such a mess, but I'm just so grateful Jesus saved me. I really don't feel like I should ever ask for anything else from Him." Is this ever your internal self-talk you do with yourself? Yet God as a Father doesn't say, "Well, yes, I delivered you of so much of a mess that you were that I think that's about all I can do for you." No, that's not God talking but some other voice inside of us.

What our Father-God speaks to us is, "I want more for your life, much more! You are made in My very Image. You're a delight to Me. I desire more for you. It is nothing you can earn. I just want to give more to you because you are My precious child!"
There's a statement that Jesus made about walking with God, and it was this: *"I have come that they may have life and have it more abundantly"* (**John 10:10**) Have you ever mulled over that statement an abundant life goes beyond just a normal everyday life, beyond what everyone else experiences.

It means a fullness of the expression of life in every dimension. Jesus came so we would have the fullness of life in every way possible. Now when we're not experiencing this fullness of life in some area,

God wants us to dance with Him, and pursue Him as a Father. We are to ask "Why is there not abundance in this area of our life? Why is our soul not prospering? Why are our children not prospering? What's going on that in our role as a father that this is not connecting? How did I start understanding how to ask God these kinds of questions about obtaining more fullness in life? When we started having children, I remember one Father's Day, Amanda, my older daughter, was four years old. We were in a church that day, and they were acknowledging fathers, and I had my arm around my daughter's shoulders. It dawns on me all of a sudden that I'm actually a father. I've had been a father for four years.

I had three children in all. All of a sudden, it grips me that I'm not just functioning as a father, I actually am a father. All of a sudden, my heart breaks wide open for my children, and I realize what an honor to be given this responsibility. Since I had no modeling of this when I was growing up, I didn't know that there was this kind of joy in fathering children. When a culture talks about children, you can have them but you don't know how to manage them or relate to them in the

Embraced by the Father's Love

best way. They can even feel like a pain in the neck at times. So we can slip into a gear where we want to get them through the teenage years, and hope they somehow turn out all right, when they finally, magically become adults.

None of that's biblical, and none of that's even healthy. The reality is that as adult men and women, we have been given the great honor of having children it is an expression of God shooting beautiful arrows of His love back to you as you raise them. (See **Psalms 127:4,5**)

TIPS ON PARENTING FROM THE PERFECT PARENT

My children have helped show me what God is like as a Father, as they relate to me as their father. Let me share a couple steps here. Because I didn't know how to raise children, a lot of my prayer life when my children were growing up was just asking for wisdom, as in claiming **James 1:5** a lot. I just didn't know what to do. The Lord would talked to me about the necessity of playing with my children.

So when they were young, I would come home

from work, usually taking about an hour on the commute. During that hour's drive. I would usually listen to the Bible, or listen to the radio. But then the Lord said, "Stop doing that. I want you to pray on the way home.

On the way home, I don't want you to pray to Me by talking to Me like you usually do. I want you to listen - it is still prayer. It's called listening-prayer, and I want to talk to you about what's going on with each one of your children and in your wife's life.

When you go home, it's not their job for them to serve you. It's your job to serve them." Have you ever heard anything like this from the Lord? And have you ever complained back to Him something like "Well, God, I worked all day long. I mean, seriously?" I then realized, "Well, okay. If God's saying this is my responsibility then He's going to give me grace to do this." So on the way home God told me how important it was for my children to play with me. So the first few years until they were too old to do this, my body couldn't withstand it anymore, I'd literally walk in the door with my documents from work, and throw them on the ground. There was usually a blanket by the door. I would take the blanket and throw it over me, and then fall on my knees, ready for some childish fun with my children.

Wherever the kids were in the house, I'd hear this shout out, "Yeah, dad's home!" Well, what that meant was a moveable playground had just showed up in the house. So they would come from wherever they were in the house running, and jump with full force into my body because I had the blanket on.

Then they would jump all over me and generally beat me up. We did that for quite a while until I had bruises all over my body, but so what? That's what it means to be a father. There was a profound joy in doing this. Then the Lord began communicating something in addition. "Brian, you need to take each one of your children every night, and sit them down. You need to talk with them, hear their heart, and nurture them."

Now, I'm not naturally touchy-feely like that. I'm more systematic and can live inside my own head. That is just who I am as a person. So God, as a matter of fact, had to spell it out to me in more detail, "This is how you do it." As I engaged in all this, I would sit down with my children, and we would really talk with each other heart to heart about life. My daughters and I really liked one another. My son actually wanted to talk with me, so I would sit down with him in his bedroom, and we would build stuff with Legos.

I have built so many amazing things with Legos. In fact, I miss those Legos. I actually can't wait until I have grandkids so I can start back up because I was building some really cool things.

Chapter Two

The Embrace of the Father

There is another very important theme of God being a Father. When we use the term "father" in both the Hebrew and the Greek, we find that it not only means "initiator", that is, someone that brings something to birth. The term also means "one who nurtures."

FATHER-GOD AS BOTH AN INITIATOR AND A NURTURER
Here on full display is the dual aspects of God being a Father. He is not only the Father who has created us and made us in His very image, and if we come to the Lord Jesus Christ, He also becomes our Father in

a unique way in salvation. He doesn't just bring us to birth and then leave us as orphans. He actually becomes a nurturing Father to every one of His precious children. So, we're going to communicate about a very important issue of how Father-God nurtures us. It is called the embrace of God.

A lot of what we call "Christian theology," that is various teachings in the Body of Christ, comes out of trying to explain the knowledge of God. This is the study of who God is, what He is like in His nature and character. Basically, in this process we intentionally do an overview of who He is, perfect in all His ways.

It is important to have a correct, mental understanding of God's nature. But as we go along, as we begin to study theology in a more organized way, there is something that seems to be too often missing when it comes to the idea of God encountering us, making Himself known to us, embracing us, and the transformation that comes from only this missing reality.

What we seem to have in the church today is a lot of people who have God-thoughts and God knowledge in their heads but too often that's about it. What we begin to realize is that there is a woeful absence of experiencing the actual embrace of Father-God. When there is an absence of this embrace, the restoration of who we are in Christ doesn't take effect in fullness. There is no spiritual fruit of peace without this embrace of God.

TRANSFORMATION BY TRUTH

In my own journey, I found that as I was trying to be restored from a history with a broken family. I heard comments of God being a loving God but I could tell in my heart that I was absolutely disconnected with the practical reality of this truth. "What is that actually like?" "How do I actually experience that reality outside of just having a concept in my head?" "Is the love of God the fullest dimension of love, or is it just conceptual?" There were the kinds of questions that flooded my mind.

In eternity, when we step over the line into heaven, what if we're not going to experience God's love? But what if just like a lot of the ways we communicate God's love here. It is just something we're supposed to think about, and then hope it's true, so that when we cross that line, we're just rookies at it?

If we're experiencing eternal life right now as Jesus taught, because we know the Lord Jesus Christ, what we will experience when we step over that line into eternity is a reality right now! The only thing we drop off then, that is different right now, will be our mortal flesh. The same quality of experiencing God forever starts the day we meet the Lord Jesus Christ.

The embrace of God is available now, and it is absolutely essential to recognize and cultivate it in our walk with the Lord. We all long for this. We were all created to be loved like this. God wants us to enjoy Him forever, and so because of this, we need to be asking, "How does this work in real life, and how do we recognize this embrace of God when it's happening?" as we look at Scripture.

MY FATHER'S BUSINESS
Let's go to the book of Matthew. What we will focus

on is Jesus when He was twelve years old or so, probably the same year He had been given his Bar Mitzvah. He had become a Son of the Law as it was and still is in the Jewish tradition. Meaning this is when someone was considered to have passed from childhood into adulthood.

He came to the temple in Jerusalem, and He was starting to relate to God as His Heavenly Father as an adult, not just to Joseph who was His earthly father. The Jews traveled in groups to go up to Jerusalem at the various festival times, so His parents weren't neglectful or under-functioning parents. They simply thought he must be with the younger people His age in their Nazareth group that was in Jerusalem.

But when they started to more intentionally look for Him, He wasn't with His peer group. So His parents then went back to Jerusalem to get him and they found Him at the temple. He replied: *"Don't you know I should be about my Father's business?"* (**Luke 2:49**). So even as a young man at the age of twelve, He understood the idea that God was a Father, in fact, His Father, and that He should be about His

Father's business. Here He is, as a young adult man, and He's getting ready to go do the redemptive work for mankind that He was born to do. He has been a functioning person, just doing what He needed to do concerning household chores and perhaps helping Joseph in the carpenter's shop, but now it's time for Him to step into the next season of his life of walking with God.

THE PATH TO FULFILLING ALL RIGHTEOUSNESS

There's a lot we can learn from Jesus being baptized. There's a lot of fulfillment of Scripture going on in His baptism. There's a lot of different directions we could go in exploring the spiritual meaning in His baptism but we are going to intentionally stay with the embrace of God: *"Jesus said to them, 'Let it be so now, for thus it is fitting for us to fulfill all righteousness"* (**Matthew 3:15**) Righteousness in this passage means that there's a path in which God wants people to live.

Think about this. Jesus is saying, "This baptism that You're about to do with Me is fulfilling the way that God wants His people to live before Him." So please don't miss this. A lot of people think Jesus went to be baptized by John for the repentance of sin. Well, that's the reason why everybody else was doing it.

But Jesus' baptism was not for the repentance of sin because He had no sin to repent of. It's very important that we focus on it. John the Baptist was doing his ministry of baptizing people for the repentance of sin but the baptism of Jesus is unique. It is pointing to a different type of baptism, and it is a fulfillment of something that the rest of us are to follow because this is the new path of righteousness.

So what was happening at this particular baptism that is unique from everyone else who John was baptizing? Let's keep reading: "Then John the Baptist consented, and when Jesus was baptized, immediately the heavens were opened to Him and the Spirit of God descended on Him like a dove, coming and resting on Him. And behold, a voice from heaven said: *'This is my beloved Son in whom I am well pleased"* **(Matthew 3:17)** Let's look at a couple of spiritual realities that we need to recognize in this. The baptism here was definitely the embrace of God. In fact, it was absolutely necessary for Jesus to have this before He began His public ministry and for Him to understand this covenant blessing coming from His Father.

But beyond His own situation, Jesus was blazing a trail for all of us who have this legitimate desire deep within us to embrace God and the ultimate affirmation of love that only He can give us.
Here Jesus at His baptism, is coming out of the water, and the Bible says the Holy Spirit descended on Him in bodily form like a dove, and rested on Him.

This idea of resting on Him is the embrace of God. If God had physical arms, because He's a Father, and this is what fathers are to do, they hug their children and bring them close. But because God the Father and God the Holy Spirit do not have physical arms, the only other way they could express this was by bringing their Presence the way that it is described here. When the Presence of the Holy Spirit came and rested upon the Lord Jesus Christ, in reality He was being embraced as close as He could be by the

Father's heart of love, and out of that heart His voice could be heard saying: "This is My beloved Son, in whom I am well pleased." Regarding our walk as followers of Jesus, the great Pioneer of our faith went through this form of baptism to demonstrate the reality of what connecting with God and walking with God is to mean for us.

WELCOME BACK HOME

Walking with God is a model of coming back home to a family, and the expression of coming back home to a family is being intentionally embraced by God. We are to recognize it, and let it nurture our hearts the way that it's supposed to do.

God says He is a God of love, and all of us are longing for it. But the lingering question that many of us have is "Can we actually experience love?" This question is addressed in the reality of Jesus' baptism and the other Members of the Trinity showing up on this occasion.

Jesus was the Pathfinder for us so we can know in body, soul and spirit that we can and should live with

God the Father's full approval right now. We don't have to just understand it in our heads or wait for it to happen in eternity. Can we actually experience God's love day by day in the here and now?

The answer for you and for me is a definite "Yes!" Because of either wrong modeling in our upbringing or wrong understanding of how love is expressed, to many of us still don't know how to receive expressions of love, or we close our heart off to love because we're actually afraid of being loved.

WATCHING OUR SON'S FIRST STEP

When I lived in Colorado Springs years ago, we had our infant son, Joshua. He was learning to walk, and actually, let's say it this way, he wasn't really learning to walk. He just decided one day he was going to walk.

Josh was scooting around on his hands and knees, he was watching his sister walk around, and I was watching him. This is amazing to me what he did. I just happened to be in the room that day with him. He put his hands on the couch. He had never walked before. He looked over at me. I looked at Josh and I realized, "Oh, wow! Something powerful is just about to happen. And Josh needs my approval for what's about to take place." So, I got down to his level where he was, and I said, "Alright, Josh. Come on, you can do it!" He got this big grin on his face, and he looked at me, and he put his hands on the couch and literally lifted himself up.

His legs were shaking, and while he was sitting there shaking, I encouraged him saying, "That's it, Josh! You can do it!" And he started giggling, and he moved away from the couch with one hand, and started bobbing and weaving. Then, all of a sudden he just ran into my arms. I grabbed him, and I threw him in the air, and I said, "That's my son!" And he just started laughing, and we hugged each other.

It was just one of the most precious moments of experiencing God's love between my son and me. When this happened, I thought, "Well, this is what it means to be a father — to encourage your children and call them to something and love them." Later, I was having a time in prayer and God said, "That day, you saw what it was like for Me in your life. I stand by and I look at you, and when you're doing something new or challenging, I come and I call you to Me, and I embrace you so that you'll become alive to that thing."

WE WERE CREATED TO EXPERIENCE A FATHER

We were each created to have a father who believes in us and calls us to something. We were created for this. In fact, it is such a longing that if this longing is not met by God, we will try to find the fulfillment of this longing in something else, and it will never satisfy us completely.

There is nothing of this world that can take the place of the Father's embrace in our life. Nothing. No food, no clothing, no amount of popularity, no fancy house or automobile, no other relationship with another human being.

We were all created at the very center of our being to be loved by God, and to be embraced by Him. Now, let's take a moment and just turn our attention to what happens if we don't experience an overt felt approval from Father-God? Does never having this experience mean that God doesn't love us? No, not at all. It doesn't mean that God doesn't love us.

It just means that as we pursue our walk with the Lord, we're going to end up seeing all the things that God asks us to do as some kind of trying to earn love by serving. We will constantly be working for God's acceptance and approval instead of from God's acceptance and approval. And this is a very terrible and tragic place to be in life. Isn't it amazing? There's a paradox in walking with God.

If this doesn't become foundational, and the embrace of God doesn't become normal in our lives we'll try to earn God's love by doing things, by performance. So our prayer life won't be enjoyable. Our prayer life will be a competition or a chore to try to get God's love. If we could just pray longer… if we could just pray harder. So the whole idea of what prayer was designed by God to be loses its meaning. It becomes this activity of trying

Embraced by the Father's Love

to earn something that's already ours - same thing with giving. Giving is supposed to be out of a heart of joy, but if we do not understand God's embrace and love, we're going to do it to try to buy God's love. Maybe God will like us if we give this much today?

The whole idea of expressing anything in the Kingdom is an expression that love has touched us, the Father's embrace has drawn near us, and out of this we give because of the over-abundance of it flowing out of us. <u>God's love is so satisfying, and meets such a deep longing in our hearts, that once it touches us, we stop having a poverty mentality and enter into an abundance mentality.</u>

The abundance of God's love transforms us to start living this way in this world. We can go to a hundred seminars on relationships, have a lot of money and any other material blessings, and try to learn to be generous, but we will not be truly and consistently generous until the heart is transformed by a generous Father. We are to get to the place where He satisfies us so completely that everything else is diminished in that satisfaction. We are to get to where it's not any big deal to do these extravagant things of love anymore, because we've been extravagantly loved by a Father.

MARY'S KIND OF LOVE AND RELATIONSHIP WITH JESUS

There are many levels to love. We will tend to receive whatever kind of relationship we are satisfied having with God. Let's look at where we can see this in Scripture:

"Six days before the Passover, Jesus came to Bethany, where Lazarus lived, whom Jesus had raised from the dead. Here a dinner was given in Jesus' honor. Martha served, while Lazarus was among those reclining at the table with him. Then Mary took about a pint of pure nard, an expensive perfume; she poured it on Jesus' feet and wiped his feet with her hair. And the house was filled with the fragrance of the perfume.

But one of his disciples, Judas Iscariot, who was later to betray him, objected, "Why wasn't this perfume sold and the money given to the poor? It was worth a year's wages. He did not say this because he cared about the poor but because he was a thief; as keeper of the money bag, he used to help himself to what was put into it. Leave her alone," Jesus replied. *"It was intended that she should save this perfume for the day of My burial. You will always have the poor among you, but you will not always have Me"* (**John 12:1-8**)

HOW DO PROMINENT LEADERS FALL WHEN THEY ARE BEING GREATLY USED BY GOD?

When I first started looking at this passage about Judas, a well-known Christian evangelist who was on television appearing before 1 in 5 people on the planet, and had much world-wide influence.

He got caught soliciting prostitutes, and it ruined his ministry. Any time a prominent minister falls like that, the rest of the Body of Christ asks the same question, namely, "If he had been walking with God, and God's blessing is on him, how could he do those things?" The second question is usually something like, "How am I going to be able to live a successful, victorious

Christian life as a mere layperson if a prominent instrument of the Lord can't live victoriously over sin and Satan?" So this prominent minister went through that, and it really had a profound negative effect. In fact, the media at the time viciously attacked him and really let him have it.

The media just seemed obsessed with his fall. They talked about it and talked about it some more for quite a while. They seemed to want to even destroy his family life. So I was praying one day in my prayer closet, and I was beginning to talk with the Lord, and I was saying, "Lord, my goodness. Can anyone make it? I mean, really.

Can anyone stand in the day of evil, or are we just destined to be decimated by one thing or another?" Then I even asked the Lord this question: "Can any ministry that represents You actually walk in integrity over time? I mean, Lord, is it possible to have a ministry over years, over decades, and maintain our integrity most importantly before You but also before the people, and finish well, or are we just fooling ourselves?"

JESUS HAS ALWAYS HAD HIS JUDASES

We all realize on a mental level at least that Jesus had twelve disciples, and one of them was a total loose cannon doing mostly as he pleased. He ended up betraying the Lord.

So Jesus had to deal with that. Back to my prayer session with the Lord, then in answer to my question, the Lord took me to John, chapter 12, and He said, "Now, let's start looking at this passage. I want to communicate the heart of the issue you've asked Me about." The heart does indeed include our emotions, but the heart means more.

It means everything that's going on inside of us, so when we say we want to talk about the heart, we want to talk about attitudes, perceptions, realities, emotions, all of this is considered the heart based on Scripture. So, let's look at this passage:

"Six days before the Passover, Jesus arrived at Bethany, where Lazarus lived, whom Jesus had raised from the dead. A dinner was given in Jesus' honor. Martha served, while Lazarus was among

those reclining at the table with Him. And Mary took about a pint of pure nard, an expensive perfume, and she poured it on Jesus' feet, and she wiped His feet with her hair. And the house was filled with the fragrance of the perfume. But one of the disciples, Judas Iscariot, who was later to betray Him, objected: 'Why wasn't this perfume sold and the money given to the poor? It's worth a year's wages.' He didn't say this because he cared about the poor, but because he was a thief. As the keeper of the money bag, he used to help himself to what was put in it. 'Leave her alone,' Jesus said. 'It was intended that she should save this perfume for the day of My burial.'" **(John 12:1-8)**

When I looked at this passage back then, I was completely oblivious as to what God was trying to tell me. So God had to start getting me to focus, and He asked me a couple questions, which I'm going to share.

There are three main people in this story - the Lord Jesus Christ, Mary and Judas. Also please remember that what we are reading is actually a commentary that John wrote years later knowing how the story ended. Later, people gained the perspective that Judas was a betrayer. But when this story happened, Judas was considered a true and leading disciple. We all know the end of the story now. We know that Judas ended up betraying Jesus. But with that knowledge, do not assume that Judas wasn't given the full privileges and benefits of being a disciple. Jesus fully trained him.

He was called to be an apostle, he was sent out, he raised people from the dead, and drove out demons and did all the works that all of us long to do. He got the training from Jesus to do it, but something wrong didn't change in his heart despite all these benefits and training.

MARY, MARTHA AND JESUS - OUR HEARTS ARE CHANGED BY EMBRACE, NOT BY SERVICE

Let's go to Mary. We realize that Mary and Martha are important in the story of Jesus because Mary decided, instead of serving Jesus all the time like Martha did, that she was going to sit at His feet.

Martha got upset with Mary's choice, and tried to get Jesus to tell Mary to knock it off. But Jesus response was in effect, No, this is what's necessary, and I'm not going to take this opportunity away from her.

How was sitting at Jesus' feet necessary? And what happened to Mary in that experience that would make her take her endowment for marriage, something that could take care of her financially for life if she did not get married, and lavish it in a few seconds of time on the Son of God's feet? This is an issue of how we see God, and how we walk with Him.

Judas served Jesus just like the other eleven main disciples. Judas did everything that we all long to do in an outward expression of walking with God. Judas moved in power, had authority, and saw the nation start to change as a result of Jesus' ministry. He had the privilege to experience all this.

Then he was actually given the honor of being one of the first twelve apostles. If Judas would have stayed true, he would have been in eternity as one of the apostles that will been judging the tribes of Israel. He was given an incredibly high position and precious opportunity. How can someone be given this kind of thing, have Jesus standing there all the time, reveal to him the real issues of their heart, and not get it? Well, this is a very critical question, isn't it? If we don't resolve this issue of letting God's embrace touch us, then we're going to spend an awful lot of time trying to serve God, and yet our heart is not going to be changed merely by serving God.

Too many regularly-attending people in the church can be in this category. The truth is, it's entirely possible to be lost in church by retaining this same attitude. Our heart is changed by being embraced by God, not by what we do for God. So, Judas had everything but the most essential thing.

Now Mary, by her response, showed that her heart had been changed. She sat at the feet of the Son of God, and what happened was that a connection formed between the mental information she gained and something deeper than just the mind.

Mary's heart became captivated by the love of Christ! What I mean by this is that when Mary was sitting at the feet of Jesus, somehow by this experience the love of God touched her.

It went so deep into her experience that it satisfied the deepest longing she or any of us on this planet have. Many of us just don't know how to satisfy it. It touched Mary so deeply that her whole perspective from that point on in life changed. Her perspective went from, "Should I go after everything everyone else is after?" to becoming a person who could say to herself, "I will lavish my most precious possession on this Man because He has so completely satisfied me - mind, soul, body and spirit!" We can develop such a knowledge of God's love for us that we realize our accumulation of stuff is really that - mere stuff.

Too many of us continue to be stuck with clinging on to our stuff and seeking to spend most of our time and energy in accumulating more because we still have fear that nobody is going to take care of us. We still have not reached the place of true security in the Father.

Can we still acquire wealth, and save up financial resources and give inheritance to our children as believers? Absolutely! But we don't do it from a fear-motivation that if God drops the ball, we will still have something.

We do it because God has lavished Himself on us, and our inheritance is just another way of expressing, "Here's the abundance of God satisfying me. Now I want something to be passed along into the next generation."

CHALLENGES TO LETTING GOD EMBRACE US

Any area in which we still have fear that God will not show up and be who He says He is in Scripture, shows an absence of understanding God's love and embrace in that area of our life.

The goal is not "I had a one-time experience with God coming through for me, but then it all got resolved." No, that's not how it works. Reality is we go through different seasons in life, and when pressure pushes on us, this is an invitation for the embrace of God to meet us again and again, quenching our doubts and fears because of the embrace of God in ever-changing, ever-growing ways. This is the Father's goal for us. This is the embrace of God!

When I was going through this passage years ago, the Lord said, "Brian, here's what will keep you from falling: If you let Me love you with My continual embrace." But how do we recognize it when the Lord is putting His arms around us?

When we are worshipping, be sensitive to a sense of the peace and the presence of the Lord. Do you recognize this is when it happens? This is the same experience Jesus had at His baptism. The Holy Spirit manifests His presence, not just to give us information, not just to show us that we're part of God's family though that is very important.

But when this happens, it is God literally running among us, in the midst of the congregation, embracing us! Let's make it really simple.

It's God actually hugging us and drawing us close to His heart.

LEARNING TO SENSE GOD'S EMBRACE

That is what happens when we're in a worship service. Well, what if we're reading the Bible? In **Romans 8:7** it states that the natural mind of man resists the things of God. But when we become born again, when we meet the Lord Jesus Christ, when we start understanding Scripture, or a Scripture is brought to our mind - we are not initiating this.

This is God drawing near to us, hugging us and speaking life to us. When we try to find God, He draws near to us, whether we recognize it or not. He embraces us with His presence, and then speaks life into us.

When He does this, what we do sometimes is walk away from it and it can feel to us like, "I've got some new revelation," instead of recognizing the first foundation of "I've just been freshly embraced by Father-God!" God wants to affirm to us that He loves us but we don't always get it.

This is so crucial in our walk with the Lord, that we begin to develop a consistency of acknowledging that we're actually being embraced. Why do I say this? I've shared many stories about my kids growing up. As they get to a certain age, many times they don't want us parents being around them, right? They think, "Oh, you're not that cool, parents, so we don't want you being around us or hugging us in public."

In our family this would get so extreme at times that my wife would get on one side of the house, and I'd get on the other side, and then we would say to one of our kids, "We want to hug you now," and they'd try to run to their bedroom, and my wife would cut them off, and we'd tackle them and finally hug them! This was back when they were teenagers. Now they're adults, and they want us to hug them again.

Reality is, whether they understand it or not, this is necessary. God knows this is necessary for us, His children, too. We need to have God embrace us. In worship when we sense His presence, God is embracing us! When we suddenly get an understanding of a part of Scripture, and it makes sense to us, that's God embracing us! When our minds get drawn toward the things of God like a magnet, or we suddenly sense we are to pray for someone, that is God's embrace. I believe this is God embracing us, and out of this great love, we initiate praying for someone. I think that in our fallen state, we naturally don't do this, and so it has to be the embrace of God that causes this kind of thing to happen in us.

So, what we call any Godward activity inside of us that turns our hearts to want to have anything to do with the Lord - whether to repent, to draw near, to want to grow deeper with Him all of this, whether we recognize it or not, is an expression of God coming near us. He is God hugging us and
pressing us into His heart, so that we can feel His love for us.

PARENTS HAVE THE DESIRE AND RESPONSIBILITY TO EMBRACE

Remember, when children are newborns, they are brand new blank pages. It's the parents' role to model embrace, so the child can understand it. When we as parents are hugging and kissing our children, they might have some basic instinct to want to be loved but children don't know how to be loved at first. They sleep, and they want to cry, and they want to be fed. That's the basic tendencies that they then have.

But parents are responsible for embracing them, for drawing them near, for talking to them tenderly and with kindness. We as parents do this because we're setting a foundation in them so that they can experience wholeness and understand what love is over their entire lives.

Somehow, too many of us have turned Christianity into, "This isn't what it means to walk with God." Our understanding mostly becomes the intellectual going through our heads, and it is learning paths of righteousness without the embrace of the Father. The whole idea of God being a father, and us trying to model it when we love our children is vital.

When we hug our children, when we kiss our children, when we encourage our children. This is so vitally important to incorporate into our understanding and practice, not only of loving our children, but of letting Father-God love us! My children are adults now, and they come up to me and say, "Hey, I need a hug, dad." Well, just so, as a child of God that knows Him and relates to Him, we can turn to the Lord and say, "Hey, I need a hug from You right now. I need Your embrace right now." And you know what? God is willing to do this. In fact, He wants to do this!

THE COMING OF THE PARACLETE - THE HOLY HUGGER

Understanding and experiencing more of the embrace of God can help clarify another aspect of the Holy Spirit that is not often emphasized. In John 14:15 Jesus promised the coming of the Comforter, a new name He was giving for the Holy Spirit. The actual word Jesus used here was "Paraclete".

The word is usually translated as "Comforter" or "Counselor" but it can also be accurately translated as "One who comes alongside and embraces." In other words, God is being described as The Holy Hugger!

WE ALL HAVE TIMES WHEN WE NEED A HUG

Sometimes what we're thinking inside ourselves, our

"self-talk" if you please, are things like, "I'm struggling, I'm alone, I'm scared, I'm having a difficult time!" Well, when we are thinking things like this, why not add one of the most powerful thoughts in all the world to go along with these? Why not add, "I'm going to go to my Father right now and ask Him for a great big hug!" And then just communicate to Him, "Embrace me!" We were fashioned for this.

So we don't want to allow man-made religion to mess this up in our heads. This is the relationship Jesus invited us into in the Kingdom. This is why He was willing to die, not just to forgive us of our sins but to restore us back to full fellowship and relationship with His Father and our Father! He opened the door and He said, "Come into my Father's house with full rights and benefits." One of the biggest benefits is He wants to hug us, embrace us and draw us near to His great heart of love, not now and then, but often and regularly. This is our inheritance in heaven. Never settle for living far below our privileges and benefits as children of God.

The Compassion of God

We will now focus on the necessity and incredible blessings of understanding God as He reveals Himself as a Father by showing us compassion. This is absolutely essential when understanding to the concept of God being a Father to us.

HEART REVELATION, NOT JUST MENTAL ASSENT, IS NECESSARY FOR TRANSFORMATION
It is easy and common to yield to the temptation to stop merely at mental assent of truth about God, instead of allowing God's true nature, character and power to impact us at the level of our deepest personhood. Mental assent is satisfied with an approach that tickles our brain but leaves our hearts

impacted little or changed. This is seen by an attitude that would say, "Here's what the Bible says. Here's a lot of theology. This is what we need to understand with our minds-- end of story."

Many of us are desiring something much deeper and we are saying within ourselves, "Okay, if God is full of compassion, how do we more fully connect with His compassion so that we can, not only understand it with our minds, but experience it emotionally, spiritually, and even physically?" As Christian teachers and believers, we are not just to teach philosophy as a mental exercise.

We are to seriously address total transformation in every respect as to what it means to be a human being. This goal alone constitutes the true teaching and full practice of Christianity. Anything less leaves much to be desired. So we're not just making a presentation of "Here's theology. Here's philosophy." We're proclaiming the Good News, and a significant part of the Good News is "This is what the living reality of God is like.

When He draws near us, this is what we are to be experiencing in every area of our life." If we are not experiencing how He describes Himself in the Bible, then we need to find a way to get to this experience.

WHAT IS A LEGALISTIC RELIGIOUS SPIRIT?

Let's look at how Jesus talked about this. In Matthew 9, Jesus is having a conversation with the Pharisees. Now please understand something about the Pharisees and religion in general. We hear terms like "a religious spirit" or "Phariseeism" or "legalism" to describe basically the same wrong idea. It's a misunderstanding of what it means to walk with God.

It uses rules and regulations to try to make ourselves acceptable to God as well as to compare ourselves with other people. What it creates is an atmosphere of loveless relationship with God as well as a loveless relationship with our fellow human beings. It becomes about rules. It becomes "Are you as good as I think I am in God's eyes? I'm better than you are." Those kinds of things.

That is not only immature, but it also shows a complete lack of understanding of who God really is. What is God's response to legalism? Well, here was God the Creator of everything, and He was saying "I'm going to go back to the essence of who I Am." Jesus came on the scene. He was talking with His people.

They had been walking away from what the Lord is doing. He was saying "Okay, let's go back to the basics here and learn something." He was in a Pharisee's house. People who are not members of the Pharisee club are also there and wanting to do lunch with the Lord. The Pharisees were getting upset with this. So this is the situation when Jesus says: *"Go learn what this means. I desire compassion, not sacrifice, for I have not come to call the righteous, but sinners"* (**Matthew 9:13**)
The word "desire" here is very important because, again, it means the core of what is in the heart of Father- God. If we take a sponge and squeeze it, then the essence of whatever it is full of will come out. Jesus was saying "I want you to go learn this again." When we claim we know God, but then we act

legalistically, it shows that the essence of God (who God is) is not being squeezed out or poured into our life. We are literally full of something, but it is not God. If we were, in fact, full of God, then we would welcome others into our house instead of putting up barriers to keep them out.

Think about this. Any place in our hearts that keeps us from showing compassion to other human beings means that we have created a stronghold and a wall in our hearts with which to resist the love of God for ourselves and for others. Amazingly, Jesus had to confront this false idea over and over with people who claimed that they were walking with the Lord.

In fact, some of them were the leaders of the nation of Israel which had been called to represent the Lord. But, in fact, they had created a closed system that distorted who God really is.
With any legalistic, religious system we have to perform
so many things in order to supposedly connect with God. Then everybody involved with us is exhausted simply by trying to be acceptable with God in a futile

attempt to connect with Him. People caught up in this do not see any example of God being loving in any dimension. It shows that people in this trap are completely blind to the reality of who God really is.

Now the concept that God is a loving, caring Father that Jesus introduces to us is so radical! This is why when Jesus started going around doing His ministry, some of the Pharisees wanted to kill him. It wasn't because He was doing miracles. It was because He was saying God had opened a door that everyone can walk through. He wanted them to stop keeping others from coming into it.

I believe God has set up times in our life for each one of us to encounter compassion and learn to respond to it. When He does this, His presence moves upon our heart and starts to work on us to receive the mercy and compassion of God. What we need to learn as believers is to welcome it into our lives instead of resisting it.

BEWARE OF YOUTHFUL THEOLOGIANS WHO ARE FULL OF ZEAL BUT LACK COMPASSION!

I moved to Kansas City some time ago now. There was a particular conference going on which I decided to attend. I had just graduated from a Bible College and so I was pretty sure that I knew everything worth knowing about the scriptures.

I was one of the great teachers of all mankind, don't you know? This attitude created a certain arrogance within me. I was very religious, also. Along with my biblical knowledge of the facts of scripture, I held it all with a religious, legalistic spirit. I felt like it was my job to come into the middle of everyone's situation and point out not only where they were sinning but how they needed to read the Bible and really get committed to Jesus.

Ever met a person like that? Unfortunately they are sometimes hard to forget, but not in the way they think that they are making an impression. But my huge blind spot caused me to not be able to see myself or this attitude clearly for what it really was. In my mind, I had done an excellent job of what I needed to do to be approved to be a minister. Now it was my job to straighten out the body of Christ and help them see their errors. So I attended this conference. I love how God sets this stuff up. The gentleman that was leading the conference is standing there dressed in some casual summer shorts and a Hawaiian shirt. Being trained as a minister, one of the first orders of business to being extremely religious is you just got to be dressed to the nines.

You just got to wear suits and ties everywhere you go. Sorry to make fun of this but to this day there were certain people in some denominations who are so in bondage to this that as pastors they even mow their yards with their suits on. It's amazing how our hearts want to be approved by God, no matter how misguided some of the attempts.

Every one of these man-made systems we come up with create these kinds of messes in people's thinking. This is because people are so hungry for the compassion and love of God to touch them, but they don't know how it's going to happen.

HAVING A SPIRITUAL MODEL OF MINISTRY RATHER THAN A RELIGIOUS ONE

This minister who was leading is up front on stage standing in his summer shorts and a Hawaiian shirt. And he's chewing gum to beat the band. He's talking about the healing ministry of the Lord Jesus Christ.

The whole time he's talking I was so incredibly offended with him that he doesn't have a suit on. The next thing that was really bugging me is he kept chewing gum the entire time while he's delivering the message. So you can see how religious I was then.

The first thing we learned in public speaking was never put anything in your mouth because whatever sound you make will get amplified as you speak through the PA system. Can you imagine? He was chomping on gum in front of a room with 3,000 people. It sounded like a cow. His chewing was being amplified by this huge speakers. I'm thinking "Oh, this is so bad. How does the body of Christ allow people like this to do ministry?" That's what was going on in my heart.

Then this leader gets done with his sermon. I don't even remember what he talked about, I was preoccupied with being so offended by him the whole time. I was literally enraged that this kind of public presentation was going on in the body of Christ. How dare people in America act this way in church?
I was really busy being very religious.

Then this minister says "Well, if the Lord so desires, I'm going to see if I can give some words of knowledge to some people." So he goes ahead and gives them, and a couple of people in the audience responded. He said very specifically "The Lord told me there is a woman here. You have scoliosis. If you'd stand up and come forward the Lord will heal you." He didn't say the Lord would simply minister to her and let's see what will happen from there.

He presumed to say what the Lord would do, period. He said "The Lord will heal you." So I thought to myself, now we're really coming down to it. We're going to see if this guy actually hears from God or is a big fake. Then he said, 'The Lord actually told me that

Embraced by the Father's Love

you're sitting in that section of the room there. If you will stand up, God is calling you out right now."
He just kept this kind of thing up. He continued, "The Lord is saying to you that if you will stand up and come forward, He'll heal you." Still nothing--nobody responded.

I thought "Man, this guy. How long are we going to do this? This is getting embarrassing." Then he does it a third time. He says "You're actually over in this section. You're over the age of 35. The Lord is saying please respond." He says "If you stand up and come forward, He will heal you." Still no one responds.

I thought "Okay, really, how long are we going to keep doing this?" Then for the fourth time, and he added, "He's told me that you're nervous right now."
He said, "If you don't respond He's going to give me your name and call you out in public." I thought, "You have got to be kidding me." I happened to be in that section to which he was referring.

So I could feel the tension in the auditorium, thinking to myself, "What is going on?" But then, this lady sitting only three rows in front of me finally stood up. She was shaking. At that point in my life I didn't understand anything about the manifest presence of God drawing near people and how we often respond under such circumstances. So I thought "Wow, she is really nervous." She continued this shaking. She looked very nervous. The leader was very cool, calm and collected during all this.

He encouraged her, "Don't be embarrassed. Come forward." The Lord just wants to love on you and heal you." She made her way to the aisle. She started walking, going forward. As she's doing this — this was very interesting - her back starts cracking so loud that you can hear it all over the place as she was walking toward the stage.

I thought, "I've never seen anything like this!" She got up on stage. This leader who had been offending me to an extreme degree all during this meeting, did something rather simple. As he started, all of a sudden I started experiencing the powerful nearness of the Lord. What he did was gently take her by her hand. He brought her up there on stage with such gentle compassion. Without spending too much time in giving a long story about it, one of the reasons I was so offended with the body of Christ functioning in these kinds of the gifts of the Spirit is how goofy I thought they acted when they were doing it.

I'm talking about all the body-slamming and all of the slapping and kicking and punching and hitting. I've made jokes about how ridiculous all this is.
To this day I can sometimes go to certain charismatic meetings and watch them and think "I can't see much difference between that and World Federation Wrestling." So back at this meeting-- I thought to myself concerning those kind of craziness I'd seen before, "Why would Jesus beat up on people like that?" Come on, I'm sure I'm not the only one who has ever seen said that. But this leader, he was not doing any of that. He was, in fact, very gentle, taking her hand and bringing her up on stage. He was very respectful of her dignity as a human being.

Then he very calmly encouraged her by saying "Now just relax." She's responding with "Well, I'm really uncomfortable." He said "I know you are. The Lord is here in His love. He's going to begin to minister to you." Her back had already been cracking before she got up on stage.

She was standing up there. So she can't be a plant to perpetrate a hoax in church. She had severe scoliosis and it was apparent. You could tell just by looking at her. This gentleman wasn't putting on any kind of a show. He was just reassuringly holding her hands.

"NOW HERE COMES THE FATHER"
Then he announced, "Now here comes the Father." When he said this - I don't know how to describe it any other way - she started to shake a little more intensely. And then, right in front of everybody, the bones in her back start moving around!
She gets healed right in front of all of us! I was then in a state of shock being an eyewitness to this. The Spirit of the Lord like a wind then filled my heart! I was experiencing

something, another dimension of God that I had tasted a few times before but had never understood. It was so intense that it just overwhelmed me. All of a sudden, God started having this internal dialogue with me. He said, "Brian, I don't heal to prove that I can heal. I heal because I love." When He said this, the only way I know how to describe it was like an arrow from heaven lodged into my soul.

It hit me with such intensity that all of a sudden I passed through that terrible, old spirit of religion. God empowered me to surpass it, and I saw who God really was! Then I realized, "I have to be wherever this is for the rest of my life!" I became ruined by God's compassion. Now I need to say something to you about God's mercy and His compassion in our life. It is supposed to delight us to be around this more intense reality of God.

It is supposed to make us hungry for more and more of it so that we pursue it. When people use the phrase, "Pursue God", it can sound almost generic or like a formulaic cliche,
can't it?

PURSUING GOD FOR HIS HEART OF COMPASSION

When we hear the words, "Pursue God" some people respond, "What for? I already know Him. I already talk with Him. I already hear about Him at church on a regular basis. Why do I need to try to pursue Him in a more intentional, intense way? I believe it's so that we can touch the core of His Being, and the very core of His Being is compassion.

You and I were fashioned to have the embrace of this compassion deeply and consistently and growing in our lives as we walk with the Lord! When Jesus was dealing with the Pharisees and the nation of Israel about this, what He was trying to say was, "You are missing Me, My heart, My essence, My core. All the religious activities you are caught up in with all the wrong motivation of trying to be acceptable to me is a distraction through Your religious system is really a huge distraction that is causing you to miss Me.

In fact, you're missing the best part of Me. All this effort is really a waste of time in My eyes. You're missing the core of what this is all about." Let's define the word compassion. The original Greek word is "eleos" in the New Testament that is translated "compassion" in English. It means compassion. Here's what it also means.

It means "on purpose showing pity." It also means "to demonstrate love on purpose or to show mercy." It means "to be tender-hearted or to act kindly." This is very important. So the distinction of our walking closer with God isn't, "Hey, we've studied the book of Revelation so much that we can know predict the future." It is not "We're such good Christians that we know how the end of human history is going to happen."

The idea of walking closer and closer with God as a Father is that He restores us back to tender mercy and kindness, and that we on a regular bases, begin to walk with Him this way as an expression of normal Christianity.

I believe that we go through life and sometimes we don't know why we do things. It's part of the fallen nature of humanity. God is constantly intervening in our life, answering our prayers, enlightening our hearts and minds with scripture He is not trying to convince us of something but because He's trying to capture our hearts and get our hearts used to the idea that His compassion is seeking us out.

He wants to touch the deepest part of who we are. Here is an interesting scripture: *"In order that in the ages to come He might show the surpassing riches of His grace in kindness towards us in Christ Jesus"* (**Ephesians 2:7**) Can you imagine? God has fashioned us in order to forever show us kindness. When we step into heaven we're not going to be asking "Oh well, we experienced the Lord down there on earth, but what are we going to be doing forever up here?" We are going to run into an ocean of kindness! This is what awaits us. The whole idea of walking with God is that we are going to be surrounded and enveloped by this constantly throughout the ceaseless ages. There is a tidal wave that's going to constantly come over our souls and constantly be washing us. What brings life, eternal life, to us is that we get to

constantly touch this deeper place of God's compassion. Not to be too dramatic, but perhaps some of you will sense it as you read this.
However, we have a part to play in being able to receive this deeper level of God's compassion into our lives. Fear, unforgiveness, anxiety, and the cares of this world can create blocks to it in our hearts. God wants to break open that dam so that sensing and flowing in His compassion will be consistent in our lives.

SEEING THE MULTITUDE, HE FELT COMPASSION

There's the wonderful example of it recorded in one of my favorite scriptures. A lot of people ask "What was the motivation of Jesus when He was involved in ministry?" In this passage we can see the main motivation behind all of Jesus' public ministry was compassion.

But as human beings we tend to forget this and develop our own lesser motivations when we get involved in ministry. The goal is to do ministry in step with God, not only to make sure we do the things that Jesus tells us to do but also with His motivation.

The Lord always has to back us up with His motivation. We need to ask ourselves a very important question here. What is the actual driver of our desire to be involved in ministry? We are not to just do something by habit.

What's coming out of us so that we want to do this? Jesus modeled what is the best motivation for ministry, and here it is:"Seeing the multitude He felt compassion for them *because they were distressed and downcast like sheep without a shepherd"* (**Matthew 9:36**)

This is God's motivation when He looks at every human being on the planet, not just His children who are not in rebellion to Him, but everybody. There is an eruption of divine love and compassion in the Father Heart of God that sees people in distress, beaten up, torn up, and life not working for them, and He must act. This compelling compassion just issues out of Him because of His very nature.

He can't leave us there. He has to run and pursue us to pull us out of it. I believe there's a war going on in the heavenlies. But this war is not only between God and Satan. I believe it is within each human being concerning the issue of whether or not we will let God rescue us. That's kind of a different statement, isn't it? Think about this with me.

The Bible is saying that Jesus felt compassion as His primary motivation in all His ministry and dealings with us. Well, I believe that you and I have been conditioned psychologically and emotionally within our culture to not show compassion because it's considered a sign of weakness. If we are going to be more like Christ then this has to change.

COMPASSION IS STRONGER THAN ANY FORM OF TRYING TO ACT STRONG

Why don't we take a sledgehammer and pound that un-Christlike way of thinking out of our lives and instead offer this affirmation for our own transformation into the image of Jesus? "Compassion is stronger than any form of trying to act strong." We are not strong when we are full of unforgiveness. We are, in fact, weak. We are not strong when we are full of bitterness, when we are fearful of life or of other people, or when we try to act tough. We are not strong in holding on to any of these wrong attitudes. No, this is, in fact, the weakest form of being a person.

Strength is expressing love. In fact, love is so powerful that it is the most powerful thing there is. It is greater than even death. The Bible is stating truth, that there is nothing that can stand up against God's love and compassion. God's love is aimed intentionally at you and me.

It is targeted directly at us just so we can see that it is His desire concerning us to show each of us love personally. It doesn't matter how much effort we make to try to keep this reality out of our life. God is going to win us over unless we are absolutely determined to lead a continual lifestyle of hardened rebellion against Him. Otherwise, He's a love-bearing missile set on finding and loving us into His kingdom and into this closer walk and understanding of who He is.
Here's a joyous statement. Let's stop fighting it and just let it happen. Let's let God connect with us. What if we

really want to experience the love of God but we don't know how it takes place. How does this work?

A RECURRING CONVERSATION - I DESIRE COMPASSION, NOT SACRIFICE

Perhaps you will find it fascinating that a lot of the dialogue Jesus had with the Pharisees was on this very point. So let's look at one more scripture. This was a recurring conversation that Jesus was having with them.

Can you imagine over and over again when He talked with them about how people are to worship and relate to God, as He was talking to the leaders of the nation of Israel, this would come up. So in this scripture He was having this same conversation with them again. What He was trying to do was to kill the spirit of religion before His time was up and He had to go to Calvary to die on the cross.

He really tried to get the point across that their legalistic system was not acceptable to the Lord. So what was the context of this biblical passage?

The Pharisees don't like that the people that don't know the Lord and aren't as religious as themselves are eating with Jesus. They don't like that the disciples were eating grain in the field by running their hands through the ripening crops. They considered this "harvesting", doing work which was prohibited on the Lord's Day. Jesus said this: *"If you know what this means I desire compassion not sacrifice you would not have condemned the innocent"* (**Matthew 7:12**)

The dialogue He has with them centered around what it means to have compassion. He wanted them to understand what it means. What has happened is they have set up an entire institution to keep people from God. This was done by saying that the primary thing God wants from people was sacrifice, instead of saying the truth, which was that the big thing God is actually after is to restore the broken relationship that He once had with us.

He wants to father us. He wants to nurture us. Out of this, He will produce a lifestyle in us that will be pleasing to the Lord if we will build on His foundation of compassion.

HE RESTORES MY SOUL

What if we want to experience this dimension of God, but we don't know how. How does it actually take place? I'd like to point our attention back to **Psalms 23**. It will probably be familiar to many of you. Most of us know **Psalms 23:1** by memory:

"The Lord is my shepherd. I shall not want. He makes me lay down in green pastures. He leads me besides the still waters" (**Psalms 23:1**)

But then it makes this phenomenal statement:

"He restores my soul" (**Psalms 23:3**)

If you and I were created in the very image of God and there is a compassionate love relationship going on between the Trinity - then it follows logically that we have been invited, by virtue of being created in the very image of God, to enter into that relationship dynamic.

Because of this, if compassion is not filling us, if rivers of compassion are not springing out of us, it means our soul has yet to be restored. When we read in the Bible, "He restores my soul", then what we need to do is engage God and recognize when this is not happening. We need to turn to the Lord and humbly acknowledge our need for Him to work the miracle of compassion in our heart. We need to cry out in prayer, "Lord, I need You to restore me so I can feel, experience and live with Your compassion."

UNCOMFORTABLE WITH GOD'S AFFECTIONS

Now part of my journey that I've been straightforward in sharing with you is that I grew up in a broken household.

I was thinking a while back that I don't remember a time that my parents told me they loved me until after I came to the Lord and told it to them first. This idea of communicating love, expressing love, hugging each other — all was just absent in my family of origin.

What I experienced from my immediate family and from my extended family was either formality or harshness. As far as my family of origin was concerned, being this way was a sign of being strong. It was seen as a valid coping strategy on how to live in tough times. It was seen as learning how to buck up for the system. But all of it was shutting me down and causing me to long for an embrace and expressions of love. I recognized this yearning because after I encountered Father-God with His Father's heart of love, He spoke to me personally and said, "I am a God who loves". And this ruined me in the best possible way.

"WHEN YOU RECOGNIZE BEAUTY, YOU'RE EXPERIENCING AN ELEMENT OF MY LOVE"

After this divine close encounter, I made a vow to myself. I said, "I've experienced it once. I have to experience it for the rest of my life." How do I find that avenue?" Then the Lord showed me Psalms 23:3. He said, "If you're sensing something within yourself that isn't normal where I want to show you My compassion and touch you and fill your heart, then you need to ask Me to restore your soul to be able to change." He taught me a prayer.

He might teach you a different type of prayer. He spoke to me, "Brian, I want you to pray every day that I will reveal My love to you, that you will recognize it and understand it." Every day I pray it. Sometimes I feel completely dead inside when I pray it, and I wonder if it's going to work or not. "God, would You show me Your love? Would You reveal it to me? Would you reveal my own heart to me so I could actually receive this? People go through college. People go through training courses. Well, I felt like I was in a seminar with the Lord for two years on this very thing.

When I lived In Denver, each night I watched the sunset on the mountains. Every night I would be overwhelmed by the beauty of it as God was teaching me to ask Him to reveal His love to me. Eventually I moved to Kansas City. I don't think there are as many beautiful sunsets in Kansas City, but one night we had a very beautiful one. I was walking up the hill with my dogs. I was watching these clouds of all these beautiful colors - orange, pink, even lavender with the Lord being the Master Artist blending them all together.

All of a sudden my focus seemed to become frozen on how beautiful it all was. And it caused me to take a moment and thank the Lord. When I did this, God drew very near to me and said, "When you recognize beauty, you're experiencing an element of My love. Now drink it in." When you don't know how to drink of Him it's extremely hard to try to do it. You don't know what it looks like. What I realized was that God was drawing nearer to me and that I needed to pay attention.

He was coaching me on how to enjoy His compassion. I don't know about you, but I've recognized a tendency in myself about receiving something from God. I want to receive it for about thirty seconds and then I want to get on to the next thing that I want to do. I don't know how to sit and enjoy anything for any length of time.

UNCOMFORTABLE WITH GOD'S COMPASSION

So then the Lord said, "Don't try to get out of this. Drink it deeply. Let it touch you. Don't be afraid of this." All of a sudden I realized I was actually afraid to experience the love of God because it made me feel vulnerable and uncomfortable.

I was asking myself what was going to happen when experiencing the love of God on this deeper level? As

God's love started nurturing my heart more deeply, I then realized an irony. I say I long for this but when it comes, I resist it. What is this issue within me?" Then the Lord said, "You're just not comfortable with Me being compassionate with you." I realized "Wow, that's actually true. I'm not comfortable with this. It's foreign and unfamiliar. I want to experience the love of God, but like a frightened child, it's almost like I need to be adopted. I need to be brought into a different family. I need to be nurtured in a specific way."

I realized that I said I long for the love of God, but I actually was resisting it almost every time God was trying to draw near to me. God had to teach me how to just sit and receive and enjoy His presence. "You don't have to do anything here" He was saying. "I do this as you just quietly worship Me."

RESPONSIVE WORSHIP

God taught me that worship is really a combination of several dynamics. God inhabits the praises of His people. We are embracing the Father and the Father Heart of God when we worship. There's really an exchange going on between us and God as we worship.

The Lord taught me several years ago when I worship and have a sense of His presence to just stop for a moment and celebrate that we are connecting! It is an intentional pause of expressing love back to Him and letting Him express His love to us. This is what I call responsive worship.

It involves purposefully and constantly saying to the Lord, "I need a deeper embrace of Your love." Every time I sense the manifest Presence of the Lord drawing near to me now, I focus on getting into receptive mode. He has invested some time training me in this very thing. Often I hear Him saying, "Don't just accept a certain measure of My love. Try to go as deep as you can." So just keep asking for more. The good thing is that God is inexhaustible in this. Eternity means He is going to be doing this with us forever. So we can't ever touch the limit into the absolute depths of the love of God that He has for us because there isn't any. He and His love are inexhaustible! That is difficult to comprehend, isn't it? Forever and ever, we can never experience how much God loves us. We'll just be growing into greater depths of it… forever. Are you beginning to see how difficult it is to comprehend it?

SPIRITUAL A.D.D. - ATTENTION DEFICIT DISORDER

I've discovered something in my own heart, that I have been spoiled by American pop culture with its obsession to over-stimulate us to have to keep trying trend after trend, and to develop a "That was so five minutes ago" attitude about everything including kingdom realities.

Many of us are caught up in this, trying to do everything, trying to experience everything - except allowing spiritual transformation to take place inside of us. I believe that this is what grieves the Holy Spirit. The term "grieve" is a relationship term in scripture.

God is a person. He is longing for us to be whole. He's a Father. He cares deeply for us. He wants to express His love to us and share that kind of relationship with us.

When we don't long for that same thing, it is just like if I'm a natural father and want to express love to my kids and they're too busy and off doing something else. You know, the "Cat's in the Cradle" song type of thing. Well, it grieves your heart.

I believe it grieves God when He cannot cut through our over-busyness to show us compassion so that we can just receive it as a love expression. Now isn't this interesting? The most powerful person in the universe is limited by us opening up our hearts to His love or not.

WHAT IT MEANS TO BE WEARY AND HEAVY-LADEN

For years I have taught on a much- quoted Bible verse of something Jesus said: *"Come into Me all that are weary and heavy-laden. I will give you rest"* (**Matthew 11:28**)

The Lord is again having me go back to the concept of what it actually means to be "weary and heavy-laden" I am to think about it in my own life, and as I talk with other people. Weariness has to do with carrying a burden that we were never designed to carry.

There are lots of burdens, aren't there? There are burdens wrapped up with just living on this planet. There are burdens that maybe a church group might put on us that God hasn't placed on us. I've noticed, for some odd reason, some people seem to be fond of certain burdens.

It makes some of us feel like we are really being "responsible" if we're overwhelmed. There is a falsehood in our culture that we are mature if we look distressed and burdened with weighty "responsibilities" most of the time.

So are we really being responsible if we look half dead, stressed out and full of anxiety and acting like the world is resting on our shoulders. That's the very issue Jesus is dealing with in this Bible verse.

WE CAN BECOME OVER-BURDENED IN CHURCH OR IN SECULARIZED SOCIETY

This temptation to become over-burdened can come at us in church through the religious spirit, or it can come at us from the influence of secularism in the current culture. But here's the great truth Jesus is revealing in this scripture. We were never created by God to have these kinds of heavy burdens weighing on our soul constantly until we finally are overwhelmed.

In fact, I believe that anytime one of these unauthorized burdens lands on us, we should recognize it almost immediately and say "Okay, God, come and love me past this." When tempted to take on heavy burdens like this, our response is to remember these words of Jesus, "Come unto Me all that are weary and heavy-laden."

The heavy-laden temptation is not primarily about adding one burden after another, that is, it is not always about the number of burdens we may have.

Being heavy laden is connected to emotional dysfunctions that are going on inside of us. People carrying burdens that they should not be results in their emotions being overtaxed because they're carrying something in their emotions that they weren't created to carry. We were not designed in the image of God to be full of fear, full of worry, full of anxiety and full of unforgiveness.

We were not created for that. When we allow it to happen, it wears us out. Be advised that because of the way many of us have been trained to embrace over-burdenedness, some people are coming into the body of Christ where God's Presence is on a weekly basis.

But because they literally are filling their hearts to capacity with lesser things, the presence of God and the reality of His compassion cannot touch them. It's hard to do, to stop worrying, obsessing, to lay down those burdens, isn't it? If you were raised in a family like my family of origin, you were taught to worry by nature.

If you didn't have something to worry about than you better find something quickly. God has not made us to be a part of all that all. Have you ever been around someone that doesn't worry? Don't they just irritate the living daylights out of you?

If we've gotten to where we think worry is normal, we look at that someone who doesn't, and we think, "What is wrong with them?" Worriers often start saying things to non-worriers to get them to start worrying. Worriers can't imagine someone being free from worry and yes, misery often does love company.

BEING FRUSTRATED THAT SOMEONE ELSE NOT BEING FRUSTRATED

Once my son went off to a secluded place to hopefully get encountered by the Lord. When he got back home, he was on cloud nine. In fact, I keep waiting for him to figure out that cloud nine was back there and doesn't exist anymore.

That's been several years ago and he's still on this cloud. If I'm not careful it starts to bug me. My son, Josh, doesn't like stressing out about things. It makes me so frustrated that he doesn't tend to get frustrated in the same way I do. So I try to worry for him sometimes. That's how I was conditioned to live when I was growing up so I can slip back into my default setting sometimes. When I'm around Josh and he's not worried about various potential things that could go wrong, I can start wanting him to get worried about something.

The Spirit of the Lord is constantly having to come towards me and remind me, "Why don't you let go of it instead of harassing Josh about it?" Those are not fun conversations between God and me. Then I try to remind the Lord, "Well, don't you understand that I'm carrying a heavy burden here?" Then God says to me, "You're not supposed to have that kind of burden either."

Now my son is being used by the Spirit to teach me to let the love of God overwhelm those things in my life and stop giving in to them. My son is a physical reminder of this to me constantly. Every time I try to go there, the Spirit of the Lord

Embraced by the Father's Love

meets me and says "Come on, Brian, just invite Me to embrace you and just let it go. Invite Me to embrace you." We were designed by God as a Father. Every time we walk into something that we were not created to carry, He wants to embrace us and love us past it. It's something we need to intentionally welcome into our lives because it's part of the Kingdom of God and Kingdom living, and learning to become fully actualized Kingdom persons!

The Mercy Throne of God

The mercy of the Lord is a truth that needs to be taught, not just once or twice but repeatedly until it is ingrained in our Christian experience. Basically, this truth means that God is a loving God who has chosen mercy as His primary attitude in relating to us, in order for His power and presence to touch and transform us.

As I have shared my own walk with the Lord and related His many kindnesses done in my life, I have been trying to paint pictures of what God's love looks like in the practical reality of our lives. Each one of us has an adventure in discovering the love of God. God creates Divine encounters of revealing His love to us in order to change us to be more and more like His Son. As I share some of the Divine encounters that God has arranged to have with me personally, I want to explain how important mercy is in changing us, both in the way we see things and the way that we live in response to it.

MERCY MEANS LOVINGKINDNESS

When we talk about the idea of mercy, please understand that the Bible could also translate it, not just as mercy, but the Hebrew word also means "lovingkindness." The reason the English translations of the Bible utilize words like "mercy" and then also "lovingkindness" is because the Bible contains many different perspectives so that we can understand better how the love of God draws near us.

When we address the concept of love, it doesn't always have a lot of clear meaning in our culture because we end up loving everything. "I love my shoes." "I love my Xbox game." "I love Thursday afternoon." "I love flying into Denver." We love using the term "love" for virtually everything. "I love ice cream." But doing this waters the word

down until it doesn't have the same impact as when the Scriptures give several distinct words for different kinds of love. It ends up not having any meaning at all when we keep using the same word "love".
When we use the word "mercy", it is a very similar situation.

Mercy has been obscured in our culture because we use the term for all sorts of things. We say "mercy." when we heard something that's challenging to us or to one of our friends. We name things "mercy." The biblical term for mercy means a heart of love intentionally showing kindness.

When we say God is a God of mercy, it's to convey that God is a loving God, loving intentionally, on purpose, and being kind to people as a choice. When God shows mercy to us, He has decided that the way He is going to relate to us will be in a very kind way. The mark or the sign of God's mercy in our life is that kindness has drawn near to us. It has touched us and it has molded us.

THE MERCY THRONE OF GOD IN ISAIAH 16:5

When I was doing research for this study of God's love, mercy, and grace, I came to a passage in Isaiah 16. It's a very short verse. **Isaiah 16:5**:

"And a throne shall be established in lovingkindness, and One shall sit thereon in truth, in the tent of David, judging and seeking justice, and swift to do righteousness".

God was dealing with the nation of Moab in this passage in Isaiah. He has been talking about how wicked they treat each other. As God deals with this wicked nation, the Moabites are going to start coming into the nation of Israel. Part of the judgment on Moab is that God was going to exile them, and they were going to start making their way towards the nation of Israel.

God is counseling the nation of Israel through the prophet Isaiah in this passage. He is saying in effect, "Here's how I want you to treat these people. All they've known is wickedness. All they've known is being abused. All they've known is training their children in wickedness, and so they have no standard of mercy anywhere in their life. When they respond that way, I want you to show them mercy this way. When they respond that way, I want you to show mercy in this manner." Then this passage ends up making an amazing statement.

It may seem a bit obscure but it actually has a profound impact for every generation when it comes to the idea of God's mercy. It says this: "In mercy, the throne will be established." Mercy means "lovingkindness." By lovingkindness, a throne is established.

The word "throne" in Scripture is very interesting. There are no republics or democratic nations talked about in the Bible in regards to government. There are only kingships being talked about. In kingships, the absolute authority rests in the throne.

The Bible often uses this term "throne." It's a way of expressing the seat of power, the seat of lordship.

HOW GOD ESTABLISH HIS LORDSHIP IN OUR LIVES

The Bible is coming to us with this very important lesson. God was training the nation of Israel and He's training us too. "Here's how I want you to treat these exiled people. I'm going to judge their nation because they are wicked, but when they come among you, I want you to do something for them.

I want you to show them mercy." Then He makes a huge declaration. "A throne is established in mercy." Mercy establishes a throne. The way we would understand this today for our generation is to ask the question, "How does God become Lord in our life? A lot of people might say, "Well, it gets down to God has all power. If I don't obey Him, I realize that there's going to be a judgment in my life.

I'm going to be on the receiving end of God's judgment and it's not going to go well, so I fear Him and so I must obey Him." The Bible comes along and says in effect, "Well, that's one way of looking at God. That kind of perspective about God is going to produce certain fruit in our life. The fruit will be that we're going to be basically a person who is oppressed. We're going to feel guilty much or even all the time. We're never going to feel the nearness of God because we won't even want Him to be very near to us. What's going to happen is we are never going to believe we are good enough in the sight of God, and we are going to live under the authority or the throne of fear as a lifestyle if we don't grow beyond seeing God that way."

Our current culture doesn't tend to believe in or want any Divine Judgment ever. And so our current culture needs to be asked a very important question. Does God ever judge people? Well, the short answer is yes. But when God talks about His judgments or when we talk about how God operates His Kingdom, we need to understand that God communicates something else that is strategically important that balances His judgments. God is also saying in effect, "This is My nature. This is who I really am in My innermost being and heart of hearts. I'm a God of love. My preference is to show mercy in every way I can and still be God." Judgment comes out of the idea of God's mercy. It isn't what we call an arbitrary thought. God doesn't just judge because He doesn't have anything else to do.

He judges because He does not want wickedness to grow too dominant of a demonstration among humanity and sometimes He sees that it is the only way to slow down or stop evil. The human race was created in the very image of God. God created us to represent Him. He wants to show mercy to us and through us. All of us have been created on this planet to experience mercy, enjoy mercy, and pursue mercy. This is the reality for which we were fashioned.

If Jesus is Lord of our life, how does He work His lordship and His throne into us? Some people may be thinking that this isn't all that interesting because they believe they already have an understanding that He is Lord. What they probably don't realize is that there are places in our experiences, there are places in our past, and there are places in our understanding – places in the heart – where Jesus really isn't Lord yet. More than a few of us have Jesus as our Savior, that is, we really are saved by faith through grace, but Jesus is not the Lord yet of every area of our life. And so, we need to ask, "How does He work Himself into our hearts and lives as Lord in our lives in those areas?"

GOD IS NOT A COSMIC BULLY

What we discover from Scripture is that God doesn't come down and say, "Now, look. I have all power. If you don't turn, I'm going to exact My righteous judgment against you." That's not how He becomes Lord in our life. He becomes Lord the way He describes it here in Isaiah.

He comes to us and He shows mercy in our life, and then by showing us mercy in an area of our life where our heart does not respond to Him in the correct way, He establishes His authority by showing us mercy which then transforms us. In some areas, we know the Lord. But in areas of our life where we don't understand who He is, it is God's job to come and show us mercy in that area so that we can get our heart established to expect goodness from the Lord. There is a weak theology that still exists inside too many Christian circles. I hear it a lot, and it goes like this: "Well, God worked once in my life. That was exciting but I really don't expect Him to do that hardly ever again. What God is looking for in me and my life is a kind of ritual.

I think He wants me to just be religious. He just wants me to be faithful and show up here and throw money in the offering plate and go to prayer meeting every once in a while, maybe witness to two or three people here or there." That folklore within Christianity has taken away from biblical Christianity and the real purpose of biblical Christianity. The purpose of biblical Christianity is for God to show up in our life and produce His character and what He is like.

The best and prime example of this is His Son. When He comes and does this, the trademark of a person who really knows God is a person full of mercy.

THE RECIPE FOR TOXIC CHRISTIANITY

When we've taken the Christian experience out of the love of God – the mercy of God and the grace of God –

what we've become is people of ritual and habit, and basically more religious than really spiritual. What this does is take the heartbeat of the gospel away from the people of God. All that God calls us to is to discover the mercy of God.

Either we discover God's mercy or we learn how the mercy of God touches us so we can give it away to another person. This is the real purpose to which God has called us. This is what it means to be a Christian. It's not so we can be hard and cold. It's not to be exacting. It's not to be cruel. That's what nations that do not know the Lord are like. Only in the kingdom of God is there ongoing, perpetual mercy. God wants to establish His lordship, His throne, by showing mercy in our life.

FIRST WE TRY TO BE COOL THEN IN PARENTING WE TRY JUST NOT TO RUIN OUR CHILDREN'S LIVES

As I share some more of my own personal struggles in this area, I remember one time I was going to a parenting seminar. Once you start having kids, this incredible desperation hits more than a few people's souls. When we're growing up as teenagers, we invest a lot of time and energy just trying to be really cool so we can attract the opposite sex to think we're awesome.

Then we get married and all of a sudden we have kids and we realize, "The whole time I was growing up, I wasn't thinking about having kids. I was just thinking about how could I be cool?

Now I have these creatures who are completely dependent on me, and I have to figure out how to take care of them. They're not concerned about how cool I am. They're concerned about me taking care of them. In fact, as they get older, they're tend to tell us repeatedly and in many various ways how uncool we are.

ATTENDING A PARENTING SEMINAR, OR WAS IT "THE VALLEY OF REPENTANCE SEMINAR"?

So I started having kids, and I went from being this really cool person to this person that didn't know what he was doing on the planet. It made me extremely desperate. I went to this parenting seminar. Parenting seminars and marriage seminars are often what I would call "the valley of repentance." Why is that? Because we realize that we're basically doing some things wrong, maybe a lot of things wrong.

By the end of marriage seminars and family seminars, we're usually repenting, praying things like, "Oh God, please have mercy so I don't destroy my family and destroy my spouse." That's why most people don't go to marriage seminars. Most of us know that if we go there, we're going to have to come out of denial and own up to doing all those wrong things we do.

Once I went to this parenting seminar. Where about five sessions in, I wasn't watching the speaker anymore because I was on my knees. I was just repenting of the fact that I actually brought children into the world and that I was basically ruining their lives. Out of God's mercy, the speaker mentioned that he was going to point out something that God told the nation of Israel to do in raising children. I thought he was going to point out that God instructed them, "You need to discipline your children." The Bible actually tells us we have to do that. We have to discipline our kids. But the speaker ignored any of that and instead focused on, "How are you doing in blessing your children on a regular basis?"

GOD INSTRUCTED ISRAEL TO REGULARLY AND INTENTIONALLY BLESS THEIR CHILDREN

The seminar leaders talked about this thing that the nation of Israel was supposed to do. They said that one of the ways that the children begin to understand God is by parents blessing their children consistently. In other words, God instructed the Israelites to be intentional at daily meals, at the weekly Sabbath, and at other special occasions to bless their children.

Looking at Jewish culture, the Sabbath is really fascinating because when they got around for the Sabbath meal, it was the father's and mother's job to not only sing songs about Yahweh to the children, but to basically in a sense, prophesy to their children and bless them every week. We find a pattern for the nation of Israel that God believes that children should be blessed every week. Then we see in Scripture that Jesus laid hands on children and blessed them. We also see in the nation of Israel that as fathers were about to pass away, they would gather their kids together.

The purpose of this final gathering wasn't for the departing parent to start a lament of, "You know, I'm about to die. Pray with me. It's going to get tough." No, the father of the family would make sure that before he left this earth, he gave them all a final blessing. I started seeing a pattern. Here's what I got out of what I call my repentance seminar. I started seeing that God wasn't asking me to be perfect.

He was asking me to open up a channel of His mercy by consistently laying hands on my children and blessing them! There is no way we can raise kids and think we've done a great job in every way. The world we live in, the way younger generations just starting out are, just everything about life today gets sane, rational parents realize, "Well, if my kids turn out somewhat functional and fairly well adjusted, it's all because of God, not because of any excellence on our part in raising kids." Starting when our oldest child was six years old, God got it across to both my wife, Kellie, and I that we were going to set up a standard that every night, no matter where we were – whether I was on the road or we were at home – we were going to go into each child's room, individually, and pray a blessing over them.

Now, this isn't about, "We told them to always look good in public and not embarrass us at church so we can look good when we speak in public." We had to model these kinds of things. I've noticed this by sitting back and thinking about the mercy of God. As we did this day in and day out, week after week, month after month, and year after year, I started seeing something happen to my children, a certain pattern that only comes from the Kingdom of God.

I started seeing that the very tangible mercy of God started nurturing their hearts. My children started becoming whole.

I watch my children now, and my kids don't even realize they're like this. But in constantly receiving a blessing of God's mercy, their friends come to them to receive blessing from them. Their friends really want to hang around them. It's really kind of weird. My kids bring their friends over to our house and, lo and behold, their friends want me to bless them, too.

Why is this? You and I and everyone on the planet, are, in fact, longing for certain realities in life. God has intentionally made us to want to receive mercy constantly. How does God establish His work inside my children's life? I give myself to something the Bible calls me to do, and I see it producing good fruit. I wanted to see mercy come into my children's life, so I intentionally showed mercy and prayed that God's mercy would touch them. I'm watching them blossom now, at this season of their life.

This isn't some technique we've figured out, but the mercy of God has been established in my children's life. They are merciful. I see them receiving God's mercy. And you know what? This isn't just for us. God wants to do this with you in your family's life as well!

I can't prove this theologically, but just by watching people, I can just tell when people are filled with the presence and the mercy of God to where it's overflowing. But with other people, they are empty. What do we do when we start to feel empty of the mercy of God? Show mercy to people until God's fills us back up again. That's what. When we cannot show mercy, it shows that we need mercy being shown to us. We need to be touched by the mercy of God.

We end up becoming – literally, in a sense – containers of mercy that we pour into each other so that we can become filled, so that we can give it away again. If you're giving away a lot of mercy and not receiving mercy, let me encourage you. Come back into a season of receiving mercy. Our souls long for it.

WE'VE ALL BEEN FREED OF OUR HUGE DEBT WITH GOD, SO WHY DO WE GET STINGY IN FORGIVING OTHERS?

How is a throne is established in mercy? Just how is it that "mercy establishes a throne"? Turn with me to Matthew 18. In this passage, we have an illustration about someone owing a great debt. "The Kingdom of heaven can be compared to a king who decided to bring his accounts up to date. In the process, one of his debtors was brought in who owed him $10 million, literally 10,000 talents. He couldn't pay it, so the king ordered him sold for the debt, also his wife and children and everything he had. But the man fell down before the king, his face in the dust, and said, 'Oh, sir, be patient with me and I will pay it all.' Then the king was filled with pity for him and released him and forgave his debt. But when the man left the king, he went to a man who owed him $2000 and grabbed him by the throat and demanded instant payment... And the king called before him the man he had forgiven and said, *'You evil-hearted wretch! Here I forgave you all that tremendous debt, just because you asked me to - shouldn't you have mercy on others just as I had mercy on you?'"* (**Matthew 18:23-28, 33**).

Basically, in today's money this debtor owes millions of dollars to his king. God is trying to teach the nation of Israel mercy again. He's saying in effect, "Okay. Here comes this guy. He owes millions of dollars to a king. This debtor begs the king for mercy. 'Show lovingkindness to me. Forgive my debt,' and the king decides, 'All right, that's it. I forgive it.' He just pronounces, 'You're forgiven.'" So how does the story go from there? This guy goes out in the street and he finds a guy that owes him relatively a few dollars, and he starts choking him and then he insists that the police throw him into debtors' prison.

"I'm not going to let you out until you give it to me back" is his attitude. Then Jesus asks in effect, "What is wrong with this guy?" He's trying to teach a point. "What's wrong with this guy?" Everyone goes, "Well, it's obvious. He was shown great mercy, and it should've transformed his heart to become a merciful person, but it didn't.

He took the mercy in and remained totally egocentric and selfish with that mercy." Once he made the decision to remain selfish with it, he became even more hard-hearted, and he remained the same non-transformed person, and ended up becoming even harder and more strict by-the-letter-of-the-law to another person. There are laws out there, right? In fact, A little later I'm going to show you another passage concerning the law. We're going to deal with the idea of how to deal with the law with mercy. Are there laws? Certainly there are. But laws are sustained by mercy. But there are times to forgive people regardless of what the law allows.

In fact, I would encourage you, let the love of God and let the mercy of God do the work it is supposed to do. Don't be concerned about being everybody else's judge and holding everyone to strict account. Learn to show mercy. God knows how to judge these things better than we do. God gives us wisdom on how to do it. Sometimes He says, "Don't let it go, go confront them but confront them My way." Sometimes He says, "Let it go." God wants us to be people who represent Him by showing mercy to people.

When God showed me mercy, here's what I found in my own past. I hadn't taken a moment to consider what really happened. I would feel very grateful to God that I had been let off the hook, but I thought the response God was looking for in me was to be by-the-letter-of-the-law strict with other people. It's amazing how the human heart is, isn't it? God can show us mercy, and our response can be to get even harder on other people. In my life, this is how God started working the reality of my heart needing to be changed by mercy. If God shows me mercy, I then need to learn how to draw from this mercy and live out of it. Here's how God did it. He put me in the most difficult situations to minister to people with what I considered unbelievable problems that there was no way of resolving unless God showed up and had extreme mercy on them.

INVOLVEMENT IN THE HEALING MINISTRY HELPED WITH TRANSFORMATION

God in His kindness sent me to be deeply involved in the healing ministry for a season. In my opinion a person cannot go through this ministry without our heart being radically changed because God purposes to break our heart in the process. The suffering of people is hard to observe, and it's hard to do ministry in that context. It's hard when you know God has a solution, and sometimes God chooses not to be this solution right then. It breaks our heart. It can even trigger the temptation to become angry at God.

God put me in the middle of praying for people that had unbelievable problems in their lives. I've watched God directly minister to some people, and I've watched God decide not to minister in this way to other people. I've been confused by it. It's done the work it's supposed to do.

That frustration, that anger, that angst, and trying to understand who God is in the middle of it has shown me His mercy. Just to show how God is, let me relate this story. I was in Denver, Colorado. We started ministering to this group at a church's food bank--and I asked, "What do you need prayer for?" We had about fifteen people in this group and the third person who responded to this question said, "Well, I've got this physical problem in my body." By the time we got around to all these people, everybody had reported some kind of physical problem. They were in pain. They were hurting.

It is hard to sit there and watch that kind of thing and respond with, "Wow, that's too bad. Well, why don't you go to Starbucks and get a macchiato? You might feel a little bit better. Then you can just go on and

suffer." It's hard to watch that. You actually have to learn to make your heart hard if you're going to watch suffering and not do anything in response to it.
I'm sitting there and the Lord speaks to my heart, "Brian, after they get done sharing this, you have people go into this other room. You're going to go in there and you're going to pray for all the sick people, and you're going to see My mercy show up." You know what my response was? I'm still amazed at my own heart sometimes.

I said, "Yeah, I don't know if I want to do that." The issue wasn't that I don't like praying for the sick. I don't like seeing people walk away after I pray for them and they're not better. It bugs me. I can start to think something like "Hey, I went out on a limb and started praying for people and I have expectation for healing and then there's going to be such a letdown if it's not God's timing for it yet." Well I fought through all these feelings and I obeyed the Lord anyway. This is always a good idea. What did God do? He showed His mercy. There at that meeting was this gentleman who was a chiropractor by profession. He had damaged his knees. He was, in a sense, crippled. He had been dealing with this for more than five years. I asked him later, "How's your knee doing since we prayed for you?" He told the whole group, "Well, I used to have to brace myself and wobble down the staircase." He replied, "Now I am walking like a whole person." You know how incredibly wonderful that is to watch the mercy of God do that? Watching God demonstrate His mercy is fantastic!

DON'T TRY TO BE SPOCK, WITHOUT EMOTION, BUT LET GOD'S MERCY AND COMPASSION FLOW

What does this kind of thing do to my heart? Well, I have to remember that I'm a guy in America where guys are supposed to be tough. I have to train myself to not blubber every time I see the mercy of God show up like that. You know, we've all been conditioned by decades of watching Spock, or other examples of no emotion.

When I see the mercy of God touch someone, I can tell it is softening me, and I have to let it come in and do its work without just collapsing on the ground and surrendering to joyfully sighing "Ugh," because that's what I used to do. I could hardly pray for people when

Embraced by the Father's Love

God would minister to them and they'd get healed. I would just be bouncing off the walls and rolling on the ground and crying from the elation. I'm trying to get back to my Spock-like attitude, but I so enjoy the river of God's mercy! Don't you? It's just wonderful to watch God do these kinds of things. It's supposed to cause us to respond in joy and love and appreciation for who God is. What makes the heart come alive? The mercy of God. The last Scripture I want to share addresses the issue, "What do we do about the law?"

In this Scripture, Jesus is talking to the Pharisees and He is having to rebuke the Pharisees because in all their effort and all their ability, they had become supposedly "perfect" at obeying the law. But they had shown none of the character of God to the nation of Israel. At the end of the day, we would have to say what the Pharisees had become perfect at was legalism, at trying to maintain the appearance of being perfect. That would probably be the trademark of Pharisees. He says this: "Woe to you experts in the law," you Pharisees. "You're hypocrites. You give a tenth of mint, oil, and cumin, yet you neglect what is

more important in the law – justice, mercy, faithfulness. You should have done these things without neglecting the others. Blind guides. You strain at a gnat, yet you swallow a camel"
(Matthew 23:23-24).

BEYOND SEEING CHRISTIANITY AS A DO'S-AND DON'TS LIST

Have you ever met someone that is trying to live for God, and they have not yet encountered the mercy of God at a very deep level? What happens with them is the Bible is reduced to a list of dos and don'ts along with our view of God and what He wants from us. According to this religious code, God just tells us, "Do this. Don't do this. Do that. Don't do that." When we're trying to figure out the love of God, He gives us what let's call ways to live our lives.

If we do these things, our life will be more blessed. I've noticed this to be true in my Christian experience. When I first started out with the Lord, it was about trying to find out what was pleasing to the Lord. I lived paths of righteousness intentionally. I wanted to show a response to the love of God by being righteous in my lifestyle. Is there anything wrong with this? No, this is good, not bad. But being righteous in lifestyle is supposed to attract people to us so that they discover the mercy of the Lord, not so that when they come near us and we are living in paths of righteous that we appear to be the most cranky, obnoxious Christian they have ever run into.

Please listen to my confession. In certain seasons of my life, I have been righteous, but incredibly obnoxious to be around. I have had times when I wanted to please the Lord so I've tried to live in paths of righteousness, but I woefully forgot the weightier things of the Lord - compassionate justice and authentic mercy. When some people first come into the kingdom, they run into these types of Christians.

These spiritual newcomers think, "Oh. I can tell they're trying to live paths of righteousness, but they have no mercy. What I'm going to do is I'm going to reject paths of righteousness because what I am observing has produced in them only a caustic, toxic Christianity. I'm going to go over here and I'm going to stay in the loving camp that lives no righteous boundaries whatsoever, because I'll be more full of love that way." Please realize that Jesus has not called us to extremism in Christianity either on one hand or the other. A healthy, balanced Christian from a biblical perspective, is not someone who is righteous after a certain dos-and don'ts fashion, but has no love.

But neither have we been called to become someone that just loves after a certain fashion but has no righteousness in their personal lifestyle. We are called to both be loving and to be authentically righteous in our lifestyle. Jesus is saying in effect, "Here's the issue with you Pharisees. It is fine that you did those things. You just forgot the weightier, deeper part of what it means to walk with God.

The deeper part of it is that you show justice, mercy, and faithfulness. When you do those things, you are showing what a person was intended to be like when God created them." The most authentically righteous person that ever lived was Jesus Christ. We enjoy His kind of righteousness, and we like it because when we follow His ways, we touch the mercy of God. Why would we want to be involved in a surface obedience in so many areas if, at the end of the day, we don't have any of the deeper mercy or justice or faithfulness in what we're trying to do? Why would we want to invite anybody into the Kingdom if, when they take a bite of the fruit that we're producing, all it produces is toxic deadness? We have a certain form; we have the surface appearance of Christians; we have it all supposedly, but we still don't have the heart of the Lord.

What Jesus is saying in summary here is, "Here's the full reality to which I've called you. Love mercy but also live righteously. Righteous living along with the mercy of God is what God has intended for us.

TOXIC CHRISTIANITY AND SPIRITUAL ABUSE

I never realized it until I went through it but there's this awful thing going on in certain parts of the body of Christ. It's called spiritual abuse. Spiritual abuse comes from neglecting what Jesus says.

We do everything right as far as surface rules, but we can turn around and treat people like dirt. We can manipulate them, we can lord over them, we can take their money but then not shepherd them in a truly Christ-like way. We can do all these things that Jesus tells us, "Don't do it." And then we wonder why authentic spiritual renewal tarries, why in so many places, American Christianity remains "a mile wide and an inch deep."

The lack of balance here creates caustic, toxic Christianity. Experiencing caustic Christianity causes a tendency in more than a few people to react negatively, to not understand the ways of the Lord and even at times to hate the body of Christ. Why these types of responses?

We hate it when we see the wrongness in living "righteously" on the surface, perhaps even knowing the Lord in a shallow way, but then exhibiting the character and the attitude more like Satan than God in our attitude towards our fellow human beings.

THE REAL DEAL, REFLECTING MERCY WE'VE RECEIVED FROM THE MERCY THRONE OF GOD

Remember the reality of that which Jesus called us.

If we have ever had this experience of entering into this deeper understanding of God's mercy, then we've gotten the real deal.

Then we understand what it's really like. How did God get me to come back to Him? How did God get me to love His people again when there are certain parts of it that are very outwardly righteous but when we bite into the fruit, it's more like the devil than it is the Lord? How does God do it? God is the fountain of mercy. He can and does find us in any of those broken places.

The way He gets us back to Him consistently, over and over again, is His faithfulness and His ingenuity in showing mercy in a thousand different ways!

Chapter Five

The Spirit of Adoption

Let's explore our identity in Christ, what it means and how we come into it. It is very good to revisit how God views us because in the final analysis, it is what God thinks and how God sees things, including us, His children, that really matters. I was talking with a pastor a while back about the congregation that he was leading. He shared how the people of this congregation and their extended families were
having all kinds of severe health conditions.

IDENTITY IN CHIRST AND THE SPIRIT OF ADOPTION

In this context the Lord downloaded the reality of adoption into my heart. I've pondered for years about how God has adopted the human race through the plan of salvation, but I haven't really sat down and intentionally organized my thoughts on it for presentation.

But during one particular week, as this pastor and I were visiting family members who appeared to be nearing the time when they would be going on to their reward, and we were trying to help prepare them to meet the Lord, God riveted my heart with the truth about divine adoption over and over again. Let's look at the specific phrase in Romans 8 which is one of the most strategic biblical passages about divine adoption, and how the Lord's been really trying to encourage those who are facing eternity to accurately weigh their place in the universe.

The truth is, experiencing more of the Lord as regards to His view and attitude about our adoption is valuable for all of us at whatever season of life in which

we find ourselves. *"For you have not received the spirit of slavery leading to fear again, but you received the spirit of adoption as sons, by which we cry out, 'Abba! Father!'"*
(Romans 8:15)

CRYING OUT "PAPA!"
The Lord started focusing me on this phrase, "We cry out" as I was doing my devotions and preparing for some additional teachings on adoption. Please understand as we encounter the Lord Jesus Christ, a lot of people encountering God perceive only part of what is actually occurring. They tend to describe an experience of going down to an altar, or praying with a friend and confessing their sins and asking for eternal life, and the salvation experience can seem to be in a moment of time rather than linear over time.

But from the Bible's perspective, so much more happens to us than just the momentarily exchange that many people perceive. God views us and His encounters with us much differently than many of us see ourselves and these divine encounters.
This is one of those biblical realities that God wants

to come progressively toward us to help us understand more and more of His heart towards us.

It is very interesting when we look at the concept of adoption. In the Bible, there are two ways that God talks about how people enter into His family. The first way is that we are born into His family. This is the concept that we are actually a new creation right now as believers. The Bible explains that it means more when we meet Jesus than just coming into a religious gathering and making a confession. We are being transformed. We are literally being born again. This is one concept that the Scriptures point out.

DIVINE ADOPTION IS ONE OF THE MAIN THEMES OF THE BIBLE

A second biblical concept about how God brings us into His family is that God intentionally decides to adopt us. Adoption is very important from the biblical perspective. It was not a very well-developed concept in the Hebrew culture.

The Apostle Paul writes about adoption in the New Testament in the context of how they understood adoption in the Greek culture. Paul talks about how God has intentionally adopted us.

Why did Paul pick this theme of adoption and talk about it in regards to our relationship with God? Why did Paul feel that adoption was a grand theme that the Lord wanted him to develop for our good? We need to look at how Paul and other writers pick up this theme. Because I have three biological children, I've never considered adopting. One of the privileges I've had is getting to know one of the people who has driven us around on our African mission trips. One man in particular spends all of his time helping orphan children there connect with other people around the nation so that these orphan children can have a home. We got hung up one morning when we were supposed to be at a meeting but our vehicle didn't show up. We were standing there for two hours waiting. During this break from our usual travel plans I asked him, "What is it like to be involved with adoption?" So he explained the process to me. He explained what it's like for the family, what it's like for the child, what the government requires, and the amount of money that it takes to pay for all the fees involved. Once he started doing this I realized adoption isn't this easy thing to accomplish. It is very a costly, time-consuming, intentional thing. This is the emphasis that Paul is picking up in this passage of Scripture. It says this:

"But when the fullness of time had come, God sent forth His Son, born of a woman, born under the Law, to redeem those who were under the Law so that we might receive adoption as sons [and daughters]" (Galatians 4:4,5)

This is very interesting. Paul is encouraging us to look what God has done. God has intentionally wanted to adopt us. This idea of adoption is intentional with God. God is intentionally pursuing us to adopt us. It was on His heart to do it.

WE ARE WORTH A LOT TO GOD - ADOPTING US WAS VERY COSTLY TO PAPA-GOD

The Bible presents certain concepts regarding divine adoption to us that are very important. The first one is that God has intentionally sought us out to adopt us as a son or a daughter. It was His intent. The next thing that God wants to get across in this regard is that since God wanted to adopt us, His work of adopting us has taken a lot of effort on His part.

It's very important that we understand the effort that God has made to bring us into His family because it's a demonstration of the value that God has put on us and how much He loves us! The Bible clearly states that the human race, all of us more or less, have a problem with condemnation. Some of us feel condemned much of the time. Others of us may not feel it but it is there because of human sin and rebellion against God. The Bible gives us a beautiful promise about how to successfully deal with condemnation: *"There is no condemnation for those who are in Christ Jesus"* (**Romans 8:1**)

For us to overcome shame and condemnation from knowing that we were fallen and that we are still far from perfect, God has to come to us and speak to our hearts, "I need to show you the value I place on you." Once we start to understand God's value towards us and what God is willing to do to redeem us and bring us into His family, then we can be delivered from fear. Father-God can transform us by an embrace of security as a son or daughter of the King.

God desires each of us to be secure in His household, It's absolutely fact that we are really part of His family, that our salvation not being easily purchased, will not be easily discarded. God has made a gargantuan effort to bring us into being His precious children! Let's look at adoption in two aspects, God's perspective and our perspective. Our adoption was costly for God. How do we know this? We already can see it in the Scriptures I have quoted, namely, that when the fullness of time came, God sent forth His Son, and God sent Him to be born of a woman under the law to redeem those from under the law. But there was a great cost for Jesus to come and do what He did.

REDEEMED TO BE ADOPTED
What does it really mean to be redeemed? We were redeemed to be adopted. Redemption was the price that had to be paid for you and me to become children

of God. I was amazed when I was in Africa to see so many children, needing a family, out there roaming the streets.

That particular African government exacts an incredible financial price for these children. In fact, just recently, they've doubled it. It's $30,000 or $40,000 to adopt an African child, and that's just the money that the government gets. Now, that's just my limited perspective on the situation when people want to adopt a child from this particular African country. But think about the concept of divine adoption from God's perspective for a moment. God is communicating to us what the actual cost was for you and me to become adopted. He had to pay a very high price for us. The word redemption here means "to pay a price." The biblical concept here comes from a historical context when in order to be redeemed people had to be placed in a slave market. At the market, slaves would stand up on slave blocks and people would bid on them. Now think about this. The enemy has made us all slaves. That's how the Bible puts it.

We are slaves to a lot of different things. We are slaves to sin. We are slaves to death. We are slaves to fear and doubt. So here comes God! He walks through the marketplace of the unredeemed, and He sees what the enemy has done to us. The enemy claims ownership of us and he's not willing to just set us free out of the goodness of his heart because there isn't any goodness there. The enemy has the human race right where he wants us. But here comes God! He is willing to pay a huge price so that we can be broken free from

those sins, from enslaving habits, from all the fears and doubts and hatreds that chain us. Now, here's our value. The high price God was willing to pay for us. Someone may say, "Well, I suppose I'd understand my worth if God paid a million dollars for me." No, money actually isn't the highest value of something, especially if you are God who owns all the mineral wealth on all the planets in the universe. We see our value in what we see God is willing to do for us.

He is actually willing to take His very own Son who is perfect and pleasing in His sight in exchange for people who hate Him so that He can communicate

a value system to you and to me. That's why it is shocking when it says in the scriptures:
"When we were God's enemy, we were reconciled to God by the death of His Son." (Romans 5:10)

WE ARE WORTH THE PRICE OF HIS SON'S LIFE

This is the value that God is willing to pay for us. The perfect eternal Person of the Lord Jesus Christ is the price of what God says our value is worth.
The intimate relationship between Father-God and His Son Jesus from all eternity past to all eternity future, the love that the Father and the Son have, all these realities communicate the reality of how important we are to God and what a huge price He is willing to pay to bring us back into His family. God risked all this in order to save us.

I think one of the first experiences of going towards Heaven after I die will be experiencing more of the reality of the price that Jesus has paid. Just worship Him for the fact that He would consider us, you and me, of such value that He would do this! The first thing about our adoption that we need to understand is what we mean to Him by the paying of such a price.

We are so important to Him that He has paid the highest price He could pay for us to know Him and to be adopted into His family. The next thing we need to understand about adoption is the change in our legal standing in His Kingdom that God has approved in our favor. Why do we need to talk about this?
"Because we are sons [and daughters], God has sent the Spirit of His Son into our hearts to cry, 'Abba! Father!'" (**Galatians 4:4-6**)

MORE THAN OUR JUDGE, GOD OUR FATHER LONGS TO BRING US INTO HIS FAMILY

For Jesus to bring us into salvation, whether we realize it or not, we have spiritually stood in a courtroom, His courtroom of the Kingdom of Heaven. The day that we said, "Jesus, come and be my Lord and Savior and forgive me of my sins," in reality, we stood before the court of Heaven. God, as the Bible describes it, is the Judge of all humanity, and when we ask God to do these things for us since Christ is willing to pay the price for us, God makes a declaration over our life, "Forgiven.

I will not count your sins against you." It's called justification or acquittal. This a legal term.

This is a legal reality. Adoption is different. Adoption is a family concept. God pours His Spirit inside of us, and then He causes a reaction inside of us due to Him so filling us with His love that a cry comes out of us, "Father!" This "crying out" shows a convincing that goes on in our hearts that God is for us not against us. This is a deep

divine embrace of who God is towards us. It causes us to come into acceptance of our true identity, and it causes an expression of it to flow in our lives.

We know that God has done all these things for us, but how does God work this into us right now? He draws near to us day in and day out. He answers our prayers. He meets our needs.

He is very aggressively trying to convince us of something: that He loves us, and that He is trying to get a response out of us. He is our Father. This is the most intimate term that can be given to humanity! It is now being given to us by the presence of God in our life and the work of God in our heart so that we cry out that God is not just God our Judge.

We know He is not far off or just a cold, legal Entity, but He's our Papa, our Daddy! Isn't that amazing? Jesus is revealing that the God of the universe is His Daddy and He is our Daddy, too. This reality is now for you and me, the same kind of relationship that Jesus experiences. This is what the spirit of adoption is supposed to do for you and for me. But it can be difficult to sink in because in our current culture, we have created such an over-stimulated, rapid-pace environment that many of us don't take many moments to enjoy anything, much less ponder over this incredible reality of our divine adoption.
The Bible is thereby advising us to intentionally think about our life since we've met Jesus-- the times that He has answered our prayers, the times He has touched us when we've been in pain, the times He has been there when we felt alone or abandoned.

We all acknowledge this, and we are grateful for this. But the Bible is saying we are to be intentional in considering what was being done there. Yes, God was drawing near to us in moments like these. Yes, at times it surprises us that He is actually doing these kind of things for us.

But He wants us to understand that all these encounters are what we would summarize as convincing us of something. He's trying to convince us that in His eyes, we are His precious sons and daughters. He's trying to bring a sense of wholeness and security in us.

NOT JUST IN THE SWEET BY AND BY, BUT WE CAN GO HOME - NOW

Do we think this way about heaven? When I get there, I am going to just feel so secure. It's over. It's over. Finally, it's over. Right? All the struggle, all the suffering, all the trials that we have gone through - it's over! I'm home. Well, isn't this amazing? The Bible is saying that this is inaccurate, that we actually came home the minute we met Jesus.

In the middle of all the things that we are going through now, this is the actual reality of our identity and our adoption. This, our true identity, is for now, when we go through challenges and trials. It is given to bring a sense of joy because we are already home, and our Dad is going to help us resolve all these things.

"DAD WILL TAKE CARE OF IT"

One of the most enjoyable things I remember as a little boy was a time when my parents were concerned about a financial problem that was going on in our household. I don't know where this came from in me, but I was eight or nine, and I said something like, "It'll be okay. Dad will take care of it." I remember going back to my bedroom, and my parents were worried about it.

I even said to them, "What are you guys worrying about? Dad will take care of it." I had such a confidence in my father as a provider and that he would always take care of us that when they were talking about this problem, I thought they couldn't really be serious because my dad was always there, he always did what needed to be done, and I had a deep sense of security in being home.

Embraced by the Father's Love

That's the reality God is trying to convince us with the spirit of adoption, that we are so deeply loved by Him that we're home - now.

"YOU ARE ALWAYS HOME, I AM YOUR HOME"
The incredible subject of divine adoption always brings me back to the first time I was in Africa. The second day of that first African ministry trip, when we were conducting meetings and outreaches, when I saw these children sleeping on the side of the road because they were orphans. I was looking at them and watching them. I was trying to take in the fact that here are all these children and their parents have died from AIDS, and they had no one taking care of them. They only had one set of clothes, and there they were sleeping at night in the open air on the side of the road.

That was a reality shocked to me. So later that night I was sitting down in my bedroom, and I have a mosquito net around me. I'm sitting inside it, and my wife, Kellie, and I were texting and she was asking me what was going on with the trip so I texted this to her. "The thing that really caught my attention was these orphans, and they only have one set of clothes." As I was texting this to her, I start weeping because I couldn't believe that children had to deal with this. Then all of a sudden this sense of being far away from home and from my family hit my heart. I start to weep because I missed my wife and my children, and I literally realized in that moment that I'm on the other side of the world. My family was so far away from me right now. I couldn't be any farther away from them. I felt a deep sense of not being home. I just wanted to go home after I started feeling that way. I'm laying there in my bed, and the Lord showed up with His manifest presence into that situation and said, "Brian, I'm with you.

You're already home. It doesn't matter where you go in the world. It doesn't matter what you're doing. You are not abandoned. You're home. I'm your home. You'll never have to feel like you're going to be alone because I have adopted you. You're my son. No matter where you go on this planet, it's home. You're home."

Adoption is designed by God to be a double blessing - for Himself and a blessing for us in our life because of the fact of sonship. That's how the Bible presents it. We have the spirit of the Son poured into our heart, and we cry "Abba, Father." This idea of sonship is so important because God could have decided in the redemptive story to just relate to us legally, as a judge making a legal pronouncement that we are forgiven, and simply leave us forgiven but still without a sense of being reunited in His family. But He did not. He went further, much further.

MORE THAN BEING LEGALLY FREE FROM PUNISHMENT, SALVATION MEANS WE ARE ADOPTED BACK INTO GOD'S FAMILY

But what is amazing is that God, as the Judge, has decided to acquit us and pronounce that we are forgiven in His sight and decided to do more. The more is that then God as our Father declared, "An adoption takes you home." What kind of judge does that? Think about it.

The very Judge of the universe who actually makes the decision whether we are acquitted or condemned

before Him, once He has forgiven us, He says, "Okay. It's not enough that I've now made a pronouncement of not guilty over you. I'm going to adopt you into My family. I'm going to take you home and make sure all your needs are taken care of." This is an awesome reality! God is trying to communicate a solution to something
that is going on in many people's hearts today. It is the condition of the heart of feeling like we are rejected, we are aliens, that we have no family. One of the main truths about God in the spirit of adoption is that God creates close intimacy with us and then gives us a family.

PAPA-GOD BRINGS US INTO OUR TRUE IDENTITY AS HIS SONS AND DAUGHTERS

When I talk about renewal and discipleship, I try to talk about the fact that one of the main things that God has given us is family. For a lot of people, growing up in this day and age, we have such fragmented families now - parents divorcing, and children not growing up in whole households.
It creates a sense of something missing in the hearts of men and women.

There's a real deep sense of loss of family in our culture. Yet one of the most defining marks of the kingdom of God is family. We get to come back into a family. We get to come back, not only to a Father, but to brothers and sisters. For the longing to know who we really are, the spirit of
adoption answers this longing. We are not aliens. We are not rejected. We are fully accepted, and we are fully loved, and by this, God pours His Spirit inside of us, and we cry out, "Papa!" Let us pray. Oh Lord, we come right now to open up to You, as You open to us all the time. Would You come now and embrace Your children, and let them sense Your spirit of adoption over them and within them.

I thank You that You
are pleased with Your children and You have called them home. I ask that the fullness of Your Father's embrace would rest upon them, Lord. Comfort us. Strengthen us, Lord. Let the blessing of your Father's approval be upon Your children today. In the name of the Lord Jesus Christ,
Amen

Brian Fenimore and his wife, Kellie, are founders of Plumbline Ministries, an organization based in Kansas City, Missouri, dedicated to releasing power in the Kingdom of God through preaching the gospel, healing the sick, deliverance and miracles. Pastoring for 20 years, Brian was brought forth in 1997 into an itinerant role of equipping leaders and churches.

He has traveled extensively across North America, teaching and imparting the power of prayer, prophetic ministry and destiny and healing. The author additional study materials and many teaching in video and audio form.

He was a teacher in the School of the Spirit of Grace Training Center, Kansas City, Missouri, and founder of Plumbline Training Institute. He and Kellie have been married for 25 years and three children.
For more information:

Brian Fenimore
www.plumblinem.com

CPSIA information can be obtained
at www.ICGtesting.com
Printed in the USA
LVHW041451090520
655282LV00003B/888